On Call

On Call

Devotionals for Nurses

Lois Rowe

BAKER BOOK HOUSE
Grand Rapids, Michigan 49516

To the Nurses

OF SWEDISH COVENANT HOSPITAL, CHICAGO
WHO ARE "ON CALL" FOR JESUS CHRIST
THIS BOOK IS AFFECTIONATELY DEDICATED.

FOREWORD

THE CODE for Professional Nurses, adopted by the American Nurses Association in 1950, states that the nurse assumes responsibility for creating a spiritual environment conducive to the recovery of her patients. If this is true, and I firmly believe it should be so, the nurse must begin by herself being in right relationship to God through Jesus Christ. Only as she makes provision for her own spiritual needs each day, can she be sensitive to the needs of her patients and be in a position to help them.

Miss Lois Rowe, R.N., has keen insight into the problems and discouragements which face nurses. In the following pages many routine nursing experiences assume new significance as they are interpreted in the light of spiritual truth and its application. This, plus pertinent Scripture verses for daily memorization and suggested Bible readings, cannot help but give spiritual strength and courage to the nurse who recognizes her own inadequacy and her need for a daily, intimate, personal fellowship with God.

Requests have often come from nurses for a devotional book written for their own particular needs. I am confident that many will find ON CALL a guide and encouragement in their Christian lives.

Tressie V. Myers, R.N.
FORMER DIRECTOR
NURSES CHRISTIAN FELLOWSHIP

PREFACE

IF YOU READ the suggested Bible readings daily, you will have completed the New Testament and Psalms in a year. I am praying for you as I write this, even though I do not know who you are. God knows you, and He wants to teach you through His Word. Will you stop, now, and each day as you read ON CALL, and ask Him to show you more about what He is really like? This is what I am asking Him to do. You see, it is only as God teaches you that the book will be of any value.

You may find it easier to memorize symptoms and dosages and orders than to memorize Bible verses. Yet the Word of God is part of your equipment as a Christian nurse, and the verse you are learning may be something very important for your patient to hear. Or it may change your life because you have obeyed God in some new way as you let it become fixed in your mind and heart.

Many nurses, graduates, and students, have helped in the revision of this book. I am grateful to all who have taken valuable time to read and consider and write and counsel. Particular thanks are due Miss Eleanor Edman, Miss Edna Anderson, and Miss Eleanor Flor; Miss Edman wrote the devotional for January 25, Miss Flor the one for January 28.

Lois Rowe, R.N.

*He calleth His own sheep by name
and leadeth them out.*

JOHN 10:3

". . . that you should follow his steps."

I Peter 2:21

I BATHE the tired, sick patient
And leave the covers neat,
The while I think of One who washed
His loved disciples' feet.
How often when I bandage wounds
Have grateful tear drops started . . .
To think!   I have a Savior who
Binds up the brokenhearted.

I pause by many a sufferer's bed
To shake and smooth a pillow,
(Remembering Him asleep on one
In boat on tossing billow.)
I give a drink of water and
(Almost too good to be!)
I hear my loving Lord remark,
"You gave that drink to Me."

I check trays for patients' meals,
Make sure the weak are fed.
(My Jesus spake the word, and lo!
The multitude had bread.)
Oh, sometimes in my crowded day
I think, and catch my breath:
My Lord healed sick folk just like these
In busy Nazareth.

BIBLE READING   *John 1*
MEMORY VERSE   *I Peter 2:21*

JANUARY 2

"Therefore, if any one is in Christ, he is a new creation; the old has passed away, behold, the new has come."

II Corinthians 5:17

YOU CAN START the New Year with a new life!

It's like exchanging a stained dressing for one that is fresh and new.

But it's better than that . . . for it is exchanging death for life and sin for righteousness.

Until we are "in Christ," the Bible tells us, we are dead in sin. Until we are new creations, we are useless in God's service — as useless as an empty supply cart.

God's "central supply" for the needs of the world is the Cross of Jesus Christ. There the Lord Jesus died for your sins and mine. If you will bring Him your old life He will exchange it for His new life. For your sins, He will give you His forgiveness; for your failure, He will give you His victory.

Read the verse at the top of the page again. Receive the Lord Jesus Christ as your Savior from sin. Let Him give you a new life for the New Year!

BIBLE READING   *John 2*
MEMORY VERSE   *II Corinthians 5:17*

JANUARY 3

"In the beginning God created the heavens and the earth."

Genesis 1:1

LET's TAKE this verse for the new year: "In the beginning God . . ."!

In the first book of the Bible (Genesis 3:8, 9), God called for the first man and woman. They were afraid because they had sinned, and they hid themselves. "I heard thy voice . . . and I was afraid . . ." are man's first recorded words to God.

In the last book of the Bible (Revelation 22:20), are man's last recorded words to God: "Come, Lord Jesus!"

Since the Lord Jesus died to take away our sins, we who trust Him have lost our fear of God. We no longer hide from Him.

And it is our privilege to give Him first place in every new day and every new undertaking. For every plan of our life, for every day ahead of us, let's put God first.

In the beginning God!

BIBLE READING   *John 3*
MEMORY VERSE   *Genesis 1:1*

JANUARY 4

"He who believes in the Son has eternal life; and he who does not obey the Son shall not see life, but the wrath of God rests on him."

John 3:36

YOU MAY HAVE eternal life. It is God's gift to you. The Lord Jesus Christ, the Son of God, died to take away your sins. To believe on the Son is to trust Him to do for you what you cannot do for yourself.

Read John 3:36. What warning is given to those who do not believe? What kind of life is offered to those who do believe on the Son?

Now read John 3:6, 7 and 16. How does the new life begin? How did God show His love for the world? How may we have everlasting life?

To learn what else is true of one who believes on God's Son read John 3:18. What is true of one who doesn't believe?

But what is eternal life? See John 17:3.

Accept God's gift of eternal life today. Believe on the Lord Jesus, trust Him to take away your sins and to give you, instead of condemnation, eternal life.

BIBLE READING   *John 4*
MEMORY VERSE   *John 3:36*

JANUARY 5

"And put on the new nature, created after the likeness of God in true righteousness and holiness."

Ephesians 4:24

WHEN YOU BEGAN preparing to reach the goal of being a registered nurse, there were new concepts to learn. You studied new books, and you began to learn the words of a new language. (You found that acetylsalicylic acid is only aspirin.)

Those who finish their courses and become registered nurses find that they are different persons in some respects, with different habits and ideas.

A Christian is a new person, too. There are new rules of conduct. The Bible becomes a new book as we study it in the light of the Holy Spirit's teaching. Even our conversation changes as we begin to speak more about the Lord Jesus.

When you pray today, carefully read Ephesians 4:24. Ask the Lord to show you some of the ways in which He would like to make you new *today*. Pray that your new life will make other nurses want to know Him too.

BIBLE READING   *John 5*
MEMORY VERSE   *Ephesians 4:24*

JANUARY 6

"My sheep hear my voice, and I know them, and they follow me; and I give them eternal life, and they shall never perish, and no one shall snatch them out of my hand."

John 10:27, 28

How CAN I know that I am a Christian nurse?

How do you know that you are a nurse at all? You have enrolled in a nursing course. You may have already finished such a course, and possess a certificate of registration which says, "This is to certify that .... has fulfilled the requirements . . . and is now entitled to be known as a registered nurse."

If you are a Christian, you are enrolled as one who belongs to the Lord Jesus. You hear His voice. He knows you. You follow Him.

You have trusted Him to be your Shepherd for this life and forever because you are one of His sheep for whom He died.

And if you do not yet belong to Him, trust Him today. Let these verses be your certificate of registration as one who belongs to the Lord Jesus Christ.

BIBLE READING *John 6*
MEMORY VERSE *John 10:27, 28*

JANUARY 7

"Put on the whole armor of God, that you may be able to stand against the wiles of the devil."

Ephesians 6:11

SUCH PATCHED and ragged Christian nurses we are, sometimes! Somebody's unkindness tears a hole in our self-respect, and we patch up the place with a big piece of bitterness. Injustice and unfairness wear a threadbare place in our love for others, and we sew it up with great stitches of growling, scolding and unhappiness. We mend the seam someone's thoughtlessness ripped; we use cross words and anger, and it makes a rough unsightly edge. Overtime and fatigue fade the colors in the shining happiness we once wore, and we put on a false dye of brittle fun and laughter at the expense of others or wear our old tired colors until people say, "If that's a Christian, I don't want to be one!"

Jesus Christ should be our dress as King's children, our armor as His soldiers. Every time we are hurt or offended or weak or tired, every time we fail or are tempted to irritation or lack of love, that is the time to take Christ as ours for just that need. Since "in every way you were enriched in Him," there is no need to dress like paupers in rags. For your uniform today, "put on the Lord Jesus Christ."

BIBLE READING *John 7*
MEMORY VERSE *Ephesians 6:11*

JANUARY 8

"Do not marvel that I said to you, 'You must be born anew.' "

John 3:7

I LOVE to work in the nursery. New lives, everything ahead for each one, inspires me. Each baby has his own individuality, each his own minute features, each has certain family traits which will grow more noticeable as he grows older.

God's children must be born into His family, too. The Lord Jesus said, "You must be born anew." You can be born again to begin an entirely new life by trusting the Lord Jesus Christ to take away your sins and bring you into God's family. There is no other way to become a child of God. You must be born into His family. "No one," Jesus said, "comes to the Father, but by me" (John 14:6).

How can one enter the kingdom of God? See John 3:3, 5.

Now read I Peter 1:23 to find out how the new birth begins.

There are endless possibilities ahead for each new baby. It's exciting to wonder what this baby will grow up to do and be. When you are born into God's family, there are some characteristics of your new life that you will want to read about, too. Look at I John 2:29, 3:9, 4:7, 5:1, 4, 18. Pray that you will grow more like your Father in these respects.

Some aspects of human genetics and birth are beyond the understanding of even the wisest physicians. God has planned birth. And God has planned the new birth. You may have a new birth if you will trust in the Lord Jesus Christ today.

BIBLE READING   *John 8*
MEMORY VERSE   *John 3:7*

JANUARY 9

"But to all who received him, who believed in his name, he gave power to become children of God."

John 1:12

ARE YOU EVER discouraged because you're not strong enough to be what you know a Christian nurse should be? Do you feel that you need more power and strength than you have? God promises to supply the strength you need today: "But to all who received him, . . . he gave power to become children of God." (And in case you don't understand what receiving Jesus means, God adds "to all . . . who believed in his name.")

Receive Him, as you receive doctors when they come with orders and directions for your work; receive Him, as you receive a welcome guest in your home; receive Him, as you receive the one you love most into your heart and life.

Believe on His name. . . . His name is Jesus, the Savior; His name is Emmanuel, God with us; His name is Lord, the One with every right to our love and obedience and worship.

And when you have believed on His name and received Him, remember to pray for all the nurses who are new Christians. Nurses know their own tests and difficulties; they also know it is possible to triumph in Christ even in those hospital situations where He is least owned. "Pray one for another . . . ."

BIBLE READING *John 9*
MEMORY VERSE *John 1:12*

JANUARY 10

"Beloved, we are God's children now; it does not yet appear what we shall be, but we know that when he appears we shall be like him, for we shall see him as he is."

I John 3:2

WORKING IN the maternity unit is thrilling. A child is born, a new life appears, "fearfully and wonderfully made." The mother asks breathlessly, "Does he look like his dad?" and then rests after looking lovingly at her son.

In the maternity unit (as in every hospital experience), God has things to teach a Christian nurse. He chose a human mother for His Son. Do you pray for these mothers? Read John 3:3. Many of them may know nothing of His kingdom and the second birth, that spiritual birth into God's family which you have experienced through Jesus Christ.

Then too, as you watch the babies eat and sleep, think of the way you grow spiritually. Look up I Peter 2:2. What things contribute to the growth of a child of God?

BIBLE READING   *John 10*
MEMORY VERSE   *I John 3:2*

JANUARY 11

"Jesus said to her, I am the resurrection and the life; he who believes in me, though he die, yet shall he live, and whoever lives and believes in me shall never die. Do you believe this?"

John 11:25, 26

HAVE YOU SEEN a family grieve over a patient who has died? Then you can understand Martha's grief. Why hadn't the Lord Jesus come when she and Mary sent for Him? If only . . . . "Lord, if you had been here, my brother would not have died."

When we are faced with grief and death, often the troubled "why?" of doubt and the "if only . . ." of regret are there. Then is the time to cling to what we know and to bring our doubts and our regrets to Jesus. "And even now I know that whatever you ask from God, God will give you." The Lord Jesus answered her with the timeless words of comfort: "I am the resurrection and the life . . . ."

There is no answer to the problem of death except the Lord Jesus Christ. To know Him is to have the assurance that death has become a "valley of the shadow" that leads to His presence, rather than a place of terror. Do you know Him?

BIBLE READING   *John 11*
MEMORY VERSE   *John 11:25, 26*

JANUARY 12

"And Pethahiah . . . was at the king's hand in all matters concerning the people."

Nehemiah 11:24

PETHAHIAH'S NAME probably means "freed by Jehovah." He was set free to serve. He was near the king for service to the people.

Nearness to our King is the only place of usefulness for Christian nurses. As a scrub nurse must be ready when surgery is scheduled, so a Christian must be on hand to help the Great Physician. At the king's hand . . . free to serve; free from worldly or sinful contamination, free too from the self-centeredness which blinds us to the needs of others.

Nearness to our King is the only place where we are free from sin. It is the only place where we can hear His quiet direction or correction or commendation.

"At the King's hand . . . " a surgeon's instrument, sterile, handy for healing, or a nurse's pen, quick to take orders. On call . . . for others!

BIBLE READING *John 12*
REVIEW MEMORY VERSES

JANUARY 13

". . . standing by the cross of Jesus . . ."

John 19:25

NURSES NEED good posture. So do Christians! Look up these verses and you'll find what a Christian nurse's posture should be:

Standing
  Ephesians 6:11, 14, 15

Relaxed
  John 13:23

Sitting
  Luke 10:39, John 12:2

In sleep
  Psalm 23:2, Psalm 4:8

"Chin up!"
  Hebrews 12:2

Walking
  Galatians 5:16

Running
Hebrews 12:1, II Timothy 2:22

How is your posture as a Christian nurse today?

BIBLE READING *John 13*
MEMORY VERSES *Hebrews 12:1, 2*

JANUARY 14

"And this is the confidence which we have in him, that if we ask anything according to his will he hears us. And if we know that he hears us in whatever we ask, we know that we have obtained the requests made of him."

I John 5:14, 15

MISSIONARY NURSES ask us to remember to pray for them. As Christian nurses we can sense, perhaps better than others, what some of their special needs may be.

Let's pray for their work, that new Christians will grow spiritually and that more will come to know our Lord Jesus because of the work of missionary nurses. Let's pray also that God will give them wisdom for their heavy responsibilities in the care of the sick.

Perhaps the Lord wants you to be a missionary nurse. Today would be a good time to ask Him about this.

As you pray, trust God to answer you.

BIBLE READING *John 14*
MEMORY VERSES *I John 5:14, 15*

JANUARY 15

"Finally, brethren, we beseech and exhort you in the Lord Jesus, that as you learned from us how you ought to live and to please God, just as you are doing, you do so more and more."

I Thessalonians 4:1

HAPPINESS can happen anywhere.

Sometimes a very little thing pleases me tremendously. Today a child with a dirty face held my hand tightly and said, "You are the nicest nurse I know. I'm going to mind you."

All day the thought of that child's obedience pleased me. It made me happy.

Pleasing God is like that. My obedience pleases Him. Happiness can happen anywhere. Sometimes in a hospital. Always in heaven. And happiness is the result of obedience.

"And without faith it is impossible to please him."

BIBLE READING *John 15*
MEMORY VERSE *I Thessalonians 4:1*

JANUARY 16

"He does great things which we cannot comprehend."

Job 37:5

SOMETIMES we see God's working. A wound heals, or a blood transfusion saves a life, a patient who might have died recovers — and we know that God is there. We realize that He has guided our hands to do what we could not have done without Him. Then we say, "God was good today."

But God does not change as we do. He is always good, even when we do not comprehend His goodness.

A little Swedish patient smiles at me as I care for her, and I know she trusts me, even though I cannot talk to her. "*Jag kan inte forstar,*" she says, and smiles. "I do not understand."

God speaks through our circumstances the language of heaven, and we cannot understand that language thoroughly yet. Knowing His goodness, though, we trust Him to be doing "great things for us, whereof we are glad."

BIBLE READING *John 16*
REVIEW MEMORY VERSES

JANUARY 17

"And God is able to provide you with every blessing in abundance, so that you may always have enough of everything and may provide in abundance for every good work."

II Corinthians 9:8

WITH THE SHORTAGE of nurses, I doubt if many of us go through a day without finding things that we are unable to do. Our time is limited for each patient dependent on our care. We feel frustrated as we attempt to meet the total care needs of sick persons.

Then it's good to remember that we have a Savior whose time is eternity, whose love is infinite, whose resources are endless, and whose power is not limited by any human weakness.

Study these verses to find some ways in which the Lord is able to meet the needs of your life:

Hebrews 2:18, Jude 24, Philippians 3:21, II Chronicles 25:9 and Ephesians 3:20.

BIBLE READING   *John 17*
MEMORY VERSE   *II Corinthians 9:8*

JANUARY 18

"Now to him who by the power at work within us is able to do far more abundantly than all that we ask or think . . . ."

Ephesians 3:20

THINK ABOUT this verse as you prepare to spend some time in prayer. What is that thing which seems too great to expect God to do for you? What nurse needs help *you* cannot give? What nurses have seemed so hard and cold you do not feel able to pray for them? What thing in your life is such a habit, or such a personality trait, or so much a part of your pride that you cannot seem to expect God to change it?

Now read the verse again. God is able to do more than you ask Him for, more than you are even wishfully thinking about. He can make you what you want to be. And He will, if you will let Him.

BIBLE READING   *John 18*
MEMORY VERSE   *Ephesians 3:20*

"I have said this to you, that in me you may have peace. In the world you have tribulation; but be of good cheer, I have overcome the world."

John 16:33

"And he called to him his twelve disciples and gave them authority."

Matthew 10:1

PEACE and cheerfulness and power! Wouldn't you like your days to be characterized by these? The Lord Jesus offers real quietness of heart, not just the quiet appearance we sometimes put on to try to keep others from finding out what we are really like. He gives courage in the face of real problems, and real strength in facing temptations.

A little while before the Lord Jesus talked to his disciples about peace He told them, "I am the way, the truth, and the life." Knowing Him as the truth helps us face truth in areas of our lives which would otherwise be hidden in anxiety and fear. He shows us what we are like, and then He shows us what we can do about it. This is one way in which we have peace in Him. We don't have to pretend or run away from ourselves when we can go to Him.

And we can accept His outlook on our world and its difficulties. Real trouble can be faced when we remember that He has overcome the world for us. We go to Him with our despair, and He tells us that He will never stop loving us, and some day will take us to live with Him forever.

When we most realize our weakness He is calling us to Him to give us power. He is real, and He is able to change even weak and cowardly and worried people like you and me!

BIBLE READING *John 19*
MEMORY VERSE *John 16:33*

JANUARY 20

"Cast your burden upon the Lord, and he will sustain you; he will never permit the righteous to be moved."

Psalm 55:22

THERE IS A TRANSLATION of this text which reads, "Cast the portion assigned to thee on Jehovah, and He will sustain thee." Your daily assignment is therefore of interest to Him.

Nothing you do is of so little importance that God does not care about it. No part of your assignment is too difficult for Him. You see, your assignment is part of the Lord's plan for you today.

Perhaps He has assigned to you a very difficult patient in order that you may help that patient to learn about God's love. Perhaps He has assigned to you a very difficult patient because there is something He wants to teach you today . . . perhaps patience.

Your assignment may be dull and tedious and you will need to learn to "do all to the glory of God" — even this! You may cast even tiresome, depressing assignments on the Lord, for He is interested in you.

But whatever your assignment for today may be, use it to prove the sustaining power of the Lord in your life.

BIBLE READING *John 20*
MEMORY VERSE *Psalm 55:22*

JANUARY 21

". . . but rejoice that your names are written in heaven."

Luke 10:20

THE RIGHTS and privileges of United States or Canadian citizenship are yours, and the safety of its protection. It is your responsibility to know what these rights and privileges are, and to fulfil your duties as a good citizen.

And if you belong to the Lord Jesus, you are a citizen of heaven. Your name is recorded there on the certificate of your new birth.

As a citizen of heaven, you share the rights and privileges of God's people. You have a right to His all-powerful protection. You have a responsibility to live as a good citizen of heaven, a representative of that country while you live as a stranger and foreigner here on earth.

Read I Peter 2:11-25. List some of your rights and responsibilities as citizens of heaven.

BIBLE READING *John 21*
REVIEW MEMORY VERSES

JANUARY 22

"For the Lord God is a sun and shield; he bestows favor and honor: No good thing does the Lord withhold from those who walk uprightly."

Psalm 84:11

TAKE TIME today to pray for those in positions of great responsibility in nursing. Pray for the director of nursing at your hospital. Pray for the faculty members. Pray for all persons in leadership positions.

Ask the Lord to use the many Christian nurses to whom He has given positions of leadership in the nursing profession. Pray for your professional organizations and ask God to show you what your role should be in relation to them now and when you graduate.

Claim the promise of Psalm 84:11 as your promise for today. Ask Him for good things for your profession, and that nurses in all areas of the profession will be enabled to walk uprightly and make wise decisions today.

BIBLE READING *Psalm 103*
MEMORY VERSE *John 12:32*

JANUARY 23

"But God's firm foundation stands, bearing this seal: 'The Lord knows those who are his,' and, 'Let every one who names the name of the Lord depart from iniquity.'"

II Timothy 2:19

THERE'S A GOLD seal on my R.N. certificate. Most important documents are marked with official seals. The resurrection of the Lord Jesus Christ is the seal which marks our new lives as Christians. There are two sides to this seal. "The Lord knows those who are His" is one side. What is the other side?

A well-planned day, a well-made bed, a correct procedure, a patient left comfortable and satisfied . . . we are proud to claim these as our own. "That's my work!"

We belong to the Lord Jesus. We are sealed as His workmanship. He knows us better than we know ourselves, better than the wisest counselor could. Therefore we must turn away from every kind of evil so that He may be pleased with His work in us.

BIBLE READING   *Psalm 104*
MEMORY VERSE   *II Timothy 2:19*

JANUARY 24

"He said to them, 'Because of your little faith. For truly, I say to you, if you have faith as a grain of mustard seed you will say to this mountain, "Move hence to yonder place," and it will move; and nothing will be impossible to you.'"

Matthew 17:20

THESE WORDS were Jesus' answer when His disciples asked Him why they could not cast the devil out of the child. "Bring him here to me," He said; and the Bible adds, "and the boy was cured instantly."

What do you do when you have a patient whom you cannot help? Do you bring him to the Lord Jesus? Sometimes you can bring him to the Lord Jesus through your speaking to him; always you can bring him to the Lord Jesus by praying for him. Bring your patients to the Lord Jesus.

What about other nurses? When you feel burdened about their careless lives, do you criticize them or do you bring them to Him?

It takes time to bring others to the Lord Jesus . . . time in prayer, time in a life of obedience to His least command, time in loving friendliness.

Ask the Lord today to show you someone He would like you to bring to Him.

BIBLE READING   *Psalm 105*
MEMORY VERSE   *Matthew 17:20*

28

"For he satisfieth the longing soul, and filleth the hungry soul with goodness."
Psalm 107:9 (KJ)

As YOU CARRY OUT your nursing care plan for some patient today, whose needs are you meeting, yours or the patient's?

What do you talk about? Things which interest you, your problems, your friends? Did you plan your day for your convenience or for your patient's? Are you really focusing your attention on the patient?

Your needs can be satisfied by the Lord Himself. He can meet your need for love, acceptance, belonging, companionship, understanding and strength.

Find Him in His Word, the Bible. Talk with Him in prayer. Commit your needs, and those of your patients, to Him. Let Him free you from yourself and your problems so you will be at liberty to give effective nursing care to your patients.

Consciously walk with Him and let Him show you how to meet your patient's needs.

BIBLE READING   *Psalm 106*
MEMORY VERSE   *Psalm 107:9*

"The apostles returned to Jesus, and told him all that they had done and taught."

Mark 6:30

"Philip went and told Andrew; Andrew went with Philip and they told Jesus."
John 12:22

THE DISCIPLES often told Jesus about their daily problems. They asked His advice. They asked Him to explain things that were too hard for them.

Our gracious Lord always answered them. He rode in their boat. He talked with them about fishing and farming and birds and candles and bushel baskets. He went on long walks with them and He even let them share His time of prayer. He settled their problems; He can solve yours.

Talk over your needs with the Lord Jesus today. Let Him be your Counselor. He knows all about the care of the sick. He can share your burdens today.

BIBLE READING   *Psalm 107*
REVIEW MEMORY VERSES

JANUARY 27

"Remember now thy Creator . . ."

Ecclesiastes 12:1 (KJ)

> THERE'S A NEED — have you seen it? — in nursing,
> There's an unfinished task waiting there.
> There's an opening for you . . . a good one!
> There's a place for your work if you dare.
> There's a Christ . . . have you met Him in nursing?
> He's a wonderful Helper and Guide!
> A Physician, the greatest and best One . . .
> Will you now take your stand at His side?

"I am the vine, you are the branches. He who abides in me, and I in him, he it is that bears much fruit, for apart from me you can do nothing" (John 15:5).

BIBLE READING   *Psalm 108*
MEMORY VERSE   *John 15:5*

JANUARY 28

Nurses base their actions and decisions on scientific principles. When principles are applied the result is certain.

THE OLD AND NEW TESTAMENTS are filled with principles which guide us in our daily lives.

"*So whatever you wish that men would do to you, do so to them . . .*" (*Matthew 7:12*).

Our behavior will bring a similar response from others. How often a smile causes another to smile! Our interactions with patients and co-workers can bring much pleasure if we practice this principle.

"But seek first his kingdom and his righteousness, and all these things shall be yours as well" (*Matthew 6:33*).

When caring for patients we consider the priority of individual needs, planning our schedules to meet the most urgent needs first. In the priorities of our daily lives, this principle must also be applied. As we become involved with possessions, purchases, and plans, our Lord says we must seek Him first. Then "things" will be no problem.

"In all your ways acknowledge him, and he will make straight your paths" (*Proverbs 3:6*).

Daily decisions . . . should we go here, or there? Should we choose this course, take that position, accept this date, study now or later? How can we *know* what decision God would have us make? If we give Him first place in our lives He will make the way clear through circumstances and an inner peace.

These are some principles God uses to lead us. Can you find others?

BIBLE READING *Psalm 110*
REVIEW MEMORY VERSES

JANUARY 29

"Is there no balm in Gilead? Is there no physician there? Why then has the health of the daughter of my people not been restored?"

Jeremiah 8:22

GILEAD, a high plateau where healing herbs flourished, was the land where physicians made their homes in Jeremiah's day. There was a balm in Gilead, and there were physicians there; but, because they sought an earthly cure for a spiritual sickness, God's people were not healed.

Today we have a Physician who understands our case perfectly. He has been wonderfully successful with others. How often He tells us to seek Him. How often He promises to answer us. Yet how seldom do we go to Him with the spiritual illness which only He can heal!

Read the first chapter of I John. What is God's cure for the disease of sin?

BIBLE READING   *Psalm 110*
REVIEW MEMORY VERSES

JANUARY 30

"We love him, because he first loved us."

I John 4:19 (KJ)

CHRISTIAN NURSES love the Lord Jesus. Would you like to know some reasons why? (You will enjoy noticing the prepositions in these verses as you read them carefully.)

We love Him because of what we have *through* Him: I John 1:7, 3:17.

We love Him because of what we have *in* Him: I John 3:3, 5:14; Colossians 2:6, 10.

We love Him because of what we have *by* Him: Ephesians 2:18.

We love Him because of what we have *from* Him: Revelation 1:4, 5.

But most of all, "We love Him because He first loved us."

BIBLE READING   *Psalm 111*
MEMORY VERSE   *John 17:3*

JANUARY 31

"For he is instructed aright; his God teaches him."

Isaiah 28:26

TRUST YOUR TEACHER! He knows you. He will set out assignments for you that will best suit his purposes for your learning. He knows what you are ready to learn. He knows, too, what you will need to know before the harder task next week.

Look for the lesson He is teaching you. He will help you when it seems hard. Sometimes I forget that He chooses the lesson, and try to learn something else that I want to know. It's always better to learn from Him.

Learn from Him in the difficult circumstances. Let Him teach you, too, in your joys.

Relate every circumstance and human relationship to what you know about God. Let the individual differences of your friends and your patients make you aware of things He may be teaching you and them. Be patient with the learning process, too. The best lessons sometimes take time.

What practical lessons can you learn from the circumstances God has placed you in today? From your Bible study?

BIBLE READING *Psalm 112*
MEMORY VERSE *Isaiah 40:31*

FEBRUARY 1

"And the King shall answer and say unto them, Verily I say unto you, Inasmuch as ye have done it unto one of the least of these my brethren, ye have done it unto me."

Matthew 25:40(KJ)

LORD CHRIST, if You would come to us today
And say, "I have not where to lay My head.
Behold My weary feet and bleeding wounds
And find for Me, within your house, a bed . . ."
If You would come! O Christ, how we would run
To make Your bed all ready, white of sheet!
How tenderly we'd bind Your sacred wounds,
How gently would we bathe Your tired feet . . .
If You were here, how glad our hearts would be!
When done for You, our best must seem too small.
Then the most menial task is glorified
And we would hurry at Your slightest call.
. . . Forgive us, Lord. "Unto the least of these . . ."
Whatever souls we serve, Your "Inasmuch"
Displays Your blessing on the dullest day
And gilds with glory every nursing touch.

BIBLE READING *Acts 1*
MEMORY VERSE *Matthew 25:40*

"Where there is no guidance, a people falls; but in an abundance of counselors there is safety. . . . Without counsel plans go wrong, but with many advisors they succeed. . . . For by wise guidance you can wage your war, and in abundance of counselors there is victory."

Proverbs 11:14, 15:22, 24:6

GET HELP for your problems!

One of the names of our Savior is Counselor. Trust Him to work out your problems for you in His own time. Put yourself in His hands, and remember that He uses many helpers. (The verses repeat the idea of many counselors three times.)

Time and hard work are two counselors God has used to help me with my problems and difficulties. Sometimes my anxious, worried heart keeps its problems longer than necessary because deliverance from sin waits for an attitude of carefree, self-forgetting trust in God. Listen to your Counselor and do what He tells you with your problem.

God also uses people to counsel us. A trusted friend, a pastor, professional resource people are available to many of us. Books provide the counsel of wise advisors, living and dead, and we neglect them at great loss to ourselves. Parents can be very wise counselors, just because they know us so well.

Finally, don't confuse yourself with your problem. You are a unique personality, the way you are because God, who loves you, made you so. Give yourself and your problem into His understanding care today.

BIBLE READING   *Acts 2*
MEMORY VERSE   *John 4:23*

FEBRUARY 3

"But she came and knelt before him, saying, 'Lord, help me.'"

Matthew 15:25

SOMEWHERE between a useless bustle,
A scurrying, scolding, hurrying hustle,
And a loitering, lagging stroll, too slow,
Is an orderly speed for a nurse to go.
How to gauge it? The answer's where
She steps in time to a quiet prayer;
For she neither hurries too fast, nor plods,
Who walks her way with hand in God's.

"Lord, help me today."

BIBLE READING *Acts 3*
MEMORY VERSE *Matthew 15:25*

FEBRUARY 4

"'Let not your heart be troubled; believe in God, believe also in me. In my Father's house are many rooms: if it were not so would I have told you that I go to prepare a place for you?'"

John 14:1, 2

ONCE SOMEONE I had admired disappointed me terribly. I was ready to give up in despair, for if that one could so fail and sin, who was I to think *I* might be able to live a Christian life?

At that time my father said something which has helped me ever since: "Young people are all hero worshipers, but there is only one Hero who will never disappoint you. Jesus Christ is the ideal Leader for youth, for He is perfect and He can never fail you."

He is better than all human leaders, for He is able to save from sin and keep His own people forever. He died for our sins; He rose again from the dead; and now He is living, wanting to live in your heart. Will you let Him?

BIBLE READING *Acts 4*
MEMORY VERSE *John 14:1, 2*

36

"Bless the Lord, O my soul; and all that is within me, bless his holy name! Bless the Lord, O my soul, and forget not all his benefits."

Psalm 103:1, 2

SPEND TIME today in letting "all that is within you" praise and worship the Lord Jesus.

Praise Him with your love. Give Him your heart. Praise Him with your mind. Bring every thought under His control. Praise Him with your talents and abilities. You have been given just the ability that He wants to use. Praise Him with your memory. No one else has ever had just your experience, so no one else can praise God in just the way that you can praise Him. He values your individual worship. Praise Him with your laughter . . . be happy in Him. Praise Him with your serious thoughts, and let your sorrows teach you how to comfort others for Him.

And don't forget to remember all His benefits! List some of them and then thank Him for them when you pray.

BIBLE READING *Acts 5*
MEMORY VERSE *Acts 4:12*

". . . not neglecting to meet together, as is the habit of some, but encouraging one another, and all the more as you see the Day draw near."

Hebrews 10:25

SUPPOSE you were in love. (Perhaps you are!) What would you think if the one you loved seemed only to care for you when you were alone with him? If he never said or did anything to show he liked you when you were in a group, but just ignored you, would you really believe he cared?

Or suppose he never allowed his affection to show when you were alone together, yet loudly protested how fond he was of you when he talked to others. That wouldn't do, either!

Nurses are busy people, and sometimes have irregular hours of work and study. It takes a real effort to keep a wise balance between personal devotions and group services, but both are necessary. We rush out to meetings night after night until we are too tired for our own quiet times with God; or we work until we are too tired and stretch out and forget about meeting with other Christians altogether. Ask God for practical wisdom in the use of your time. Read Hebrews 10:25 again.

BIBLE READING   *Acts 6*
MEMORY VERSE   *Heb. 10:25*

FEBRUARY 7

"First of all you must understand this, that no prophecy of Scripture is a matter of one's own interpretation, because no prophecy ever came by the impulse of man, but men moved by the Holy Spirit spoke from God."

II Peter 1:20, 21

WHAT DO YOU know about the promises of God concerning the coming of the Lord Jesus? Here are some prophecies, written many years before He came. Study them today:

Isaiah 7:14, 42:1-3, 28:16, 49:1-6, 50:5, 6; Psalm 22:1, 9-18; Psalm 24; and Micah 5:2.

BIBLE READING   *Acts 7*
MEMORY VERSE   *II Peter 1:20, 21*

FEBRUARY 8

"God is a Spirit, and those who worship him must worship in spirit and in truth."

John 4:24

THERE ARE certain requirements that go with the worship of God. You may loudly maintain your loyalty to the nursing profession, but unless you live up to its ideals you are not a loyal nurse. So it is with the true worshiper.

Study these verses: Matthew 8:2; John 4:24, 9:38, 31; Psalm 96:9; II Kings 17:36, 37.

38

List the requirements for worship which you find in these verses. Take time to worship the Lord today according to these requirements before you go on duty.

BIBLE READING   *Acts 8*
REVIEW MEMORY VERSES

FEBRUARY 9

"Let the words of my mouth and the meditation of my heart be acceptable in thy sight, O Lord, my rock, and my redeemer."

Psalm 19:14

PRAY TODAY that the Lord will help us as nurses to live holy lives in our profession. Ask Him to help you live and worship "in the beauty of holiness."

Today, pray for Christian nurses who are alone in their place of service for the Lord Jesus. Pray for those who are on lonely mission stations, for those who are the only Christians in their hospital settings. Ask that they may be given courage and faith, that God will fulfil His purpose for them.

Pray that today they may feel the presence of the Lord Jesus and be good witnesses for Him.

BIBLE READING   *Acts 9*
MEMORY VERSE   *Psalm 19:14*

FEBRUARY 10

" '. . . this thing is from me.' "

I Kings 12:24

> WE GO to the room together,
> My Lord and I.
> He takes a patient's hand.
> I try
> To do the treatments gently
> As I've learned them.
> Then
> We go together to the hall again.

"Thank you for your work," He whispers.
"Lord," I pray,
"Let me take orders on Your rounds
All day today."

BIBLE READING   *Acts 10*
REVIEW MEMORY VERSES

FEBRUARY 11

"And you shall rejoice in all the good which the Lord your God has given
you."

Deuteronomy 26:11

WORSHIP and rejoice! Worship is not meant to be sad and solemn,
but glad and joyful . . . a happy reverence. There are more than
365 references to joy, happiness, gladness and rejoicing in the
Bible — happiness, as someone has pointed out, to last for every day
of the year.

We are offended when a patient grumbles about the care we
have given him. "Ungrateful!" we sniff.

When we complain about anything God allows to come into
our lives, we are being ungrateful for His care. Nothing can
touch us except what He ordains or permits as part of His plan
to make us more like the Lord Jesus.

"Serve the Lord with gladness" today. "Come into his presence
with thanksgiving"!

BIBLE READING   *Acts 11*
MEMORY VERSE   *Deuteronomy 26:11*

FEBRUARY 12

"And the man bowed down his head, and worshipped the Lord. And he said, Blessed be the Lord God of my master Abraham, who hath not left destitute my master of his mercy and his truth; I being in the way, the Lord led me to the house of my master's brethren."

Genesis 24:26, 27 (KJ)

"THE LORD led me." Is He leading you?

Here is a man in a strange country. He is looking for a wife for his master's son, and he doesn't know anybody. What a situation!

Here is a nurse, a Christian nurse, whose real home is Heaven. She is working in a hospital, caring for strange patients; she is looking for someone who wants to know about her Master, the Lord Jesus.

The man was in the way, praying for guidance, trusting the Lord to work things out for him. And the Lord led him.

If you are acquainted with the Lord Jesus, you can trust Him to guide you to the very patient who needs Him most. He knows all the patients you will serve today, because He is planning your hours and assignments far in advance of the head nurse who writes them down.

But you must be "in the way" . . . guidable, ready to obey His leading, if you want His guidance today. Tell Him so if you do.

BIBLE READING *Acts 12*
REVIEW MEMORY VERSES

FEBRUARY 13

In II Chronicles 20 there is a story about Jehoshaphat, one of the good kings of Judah. It is an interesting story because so much of it can apply to our lives today as Christian nurses.

FOR YOUR READING today, go carefully through this chapter. See if you find the answers to these questions:

What did Jehoshaphat do when he heard that a multitude was coming against him? (What do you do when things go against you?)

Jehoshaphat reminded God of a promise. What was it? Did Jehoshaphat believe in admitting his own weakness to God? Have you ever talked to God about your lack of strength, specifically naming your inadequacies?

Where should we look when we don't know what to do? Where do you look?

What did God answer? Whose is the battle?

What is the condition given in this chapter for being established and prospering?

What happened when the people began to praise? What happens to the forces of evil when we praise God?

What happened to the world around Jehoshaphat?

BIBLE READING   *Acts 13*
MEMORY VERSE   *II Chronicles 20:17*

FEBRUARY 14

"My son, give me your heart, and let your eyes observe my ways."
Proverbs 23:26

VALENTINES! Hearts and flowers! Be mine!

Without silly sentimentality, God sent His world a serious valentine. "Give me your heart," He said, "and let your eyes observe my ways."

Sometimes we get sweets for valentines. Let them remind us to stamp on our words and doings today the sweetness of the knowledge of the Lord Jesus, remembering each moment that "I am His and He is mine."

The fragrance of flowers on Valentine's Day may remind us of the Rose of Sharon, the Lily of the Valley, the fragrance of the loving life of the Lord Jesus.

Some valentines are rude caricatures, mean and caustic, or flippant and funny. They pretend to be the real thing, but inside there is a different story.

Are you real and sincere in your life for God today? Give Him your heart. Then show your love for Him by the way you act.

BIBLE READING   *Acts 14*
MEMORY VERSE   *Proverbs 23:26*

"We know that God does not listen to sinners, but if any one is a worshiper of God and does his will, God listens to him."

John 9:31

STUDENTS who fail to conform to the policies of their school may be asking for trouble. A doctor who disobeys hospital rules isn't kept on the staff. A patient who won't follow doctor's orders will not usually progress as rapidly as one who cooperates. A nurse who fails to follow scientific principles is unsuccessful in the results she achieves.

And a Christian who is unwilling to do the will of God cannot expect to have his prayers answered. Our requests are to be "according to His will." God is very merciful, and He always does more than we expect, far more than we deserve. But a deliberately disobedient Christian is not in a place to ask God to answer any prayer except the prayer of a contrite heart.

BIBLE READING *Acts 15*
REVIEW MEMORY VERSES

" 'For this child I prayed; and the Lord has granted me my petition which I made to him.' "

I Samuel 1:27

A SORROWFUL woman wept before the Lord. She was deeply distressed. She asked the Lord to remember her, and she promised that if He would give her a son, she would give him back to God.

The Lord heard her petition, gave her a son, and she became the mother of Samuel, one of the greatest priests of the Lord.

What a wonderful story! And all in answer to prayer.

Ask the Lord for your heart's desire. If you are in His will, and pray believing, then it is His promise that some day you too can come with your answer and say, "For this . . . I prayed; and the Lord has granted me my petition which I made to him."

BIBLE READING *Acts 16*
MEMORY VERSE *I Samuel 1:27*

FEBRUARY 17

"For as we share abundantly in Christ's sufferings, so through Christ we share abundantly in comfort too."

II Corinthians 1:5

ONE OF THE SADDEST tasks of the nurse is the care of the dying. It is hard to know what to say to the patient and to his family. Today's Bible study will help you in this difficult phase of Christian nursing:

Faith and death: *Hebrews 11:21, 22*
Grieving parents: *Job 1:21*
Blaming God: *Job 1:22*
The death of Christians: *I Thessalonians 4:14*
Grieving for Christians: *I Thessalonians 4:13*
Gain in death: *Philippians 1:21*
With the Lord: *Philippians 1:23*
Why suffering: *II Corinthians 1:4*
Our consolation: *II Thessalonians 2:16, 17*

BIBLE READING   *Acts 17*
MEMORY VERSE   *II Corinthians 1:5*

FEBRUARY 18

"God is our refuge and strength, a very present help in trouble."

Psalm 46:1

ANOTHER translation reads "a help in distresses, very readily found."

God our refuge and our strength, a very present help, very readily found! What need have you today that He cannot meet? What problem can you possibly face that He has not solved long ago?

He is very readily found. As you pray today, be assured of His presence. It is a fact, not a feeling. Even as a very busy nurse, you may find Him your refuge and strength as you need Him.

Pray for nurses who are in any kind of trouble today. Pray that they may seek God as their refuge. Ask God to use you as He desires in the lives of nurses who are looking for Him today.

BIBLE READING   *Acts 18*
MEMORY VERSE   *Psalm 46:1*

"But he said to me, 'My grace is sufficient for you, for my power is made perfect in weakness.' I will all the more gladly boast of my weaknesses, that the power of Christ may rest upon me."

11 Corinthians 12:9

THERE IS ANOTHER verse that says, "For by grace you have been saved through faith; and this is not your own doing, it is the gift of God — not of works, lest any man should boast" (*Ephesians* 2:8,9).

Have you been trying to overcome your own weakness? Have you been struggling to make yourself the kind of nurse you wish you were?

Stop struggling. Turn to the Lord Jesus Christ. Tell Him about your weakness. Tell Him about your need of Him. He can teach you to trust His sufficiency for everything you need.

> I am weak,
> He is strong.
> He is near,
> All day long.
> Sing, O heart!
> This, thy song:
> He is near,
> I am strong!

BIBLE READING   *Acts 19*
MEMORY VERSE   *II Corinthians 12:9*

". . . declare this with a shout of joy, proclaim it, send it forth to the end of the earth; say, 'The Lord has redeemed his servant Jacob!' "

Isaiah 48:20

WHAT DO YOU THINK a person is like whom God calls His servant? There are some uncomplimentary things said in Isaiah 48 about His servant Jacob. God calls him treacherous, a rebel from birth, not honest, not righteous. He says Jacob is obstinate and a proud idolator.

When I look deep in my own heart I find this Jacob. Sometimes I act this way. Then I want to say that I cannot be a servant of God at all, so dishonest, so proud, so stubborn, so rebellious.

I read the chapter again. I find that the Lord loves Jacob. I find that the Lord, for His own sake, redeems, teaches, purifies, and leads him. The Lord calls Himself Jacob's Redeemer. He is my Redeemer, too.

Next time you fail, remember that the Lord loves you. Change your discouragement to a shout of joy. And when you confess your sin accept His forgiveness, saying, "The Lord has redeemed His servant."

BIBLE READING   *Acts 20*
MEMORY VERSE   *Isaiah 48:20*

FEBRUARY 21

"Then Moses turned again to the Lord and said, 'O Lord, why hast thou done evil to this people? Why didst thou ever send me?' . . . But the Lord said to Moses, 'Now you shall see what I will do to Pharaoh.'"
Exodus 5:22, 6:1

INSTEAD of the fretful "Why?" of doubt, remember the triumphant "Now!" of faith. Just at the point where we say in discouragement, "Why did You send me here?" the Lord may be about to say, "Now you shall see what I will do!"

One of the hard things in nursing is the discouraging everydayness of a load too big to bear, responsibilities too overwhelming. We meet so many things we're unable to do because we only have two hands. And we feel so inadequate.

But His strength is made perfect in weakness, even your weakness. Trust Him for today's need. You'll see what He will do!

"Behold, I am the Lord . . . is anything too hard for me?" (Jeremiah 32:27).

BIBLE READING   *Acts 21*
MEMORY VERSE   *Jeremiah 32:27*

". . . your life is hid with Christ in God."

Colossians 3:3

IF YOUR LIFE is hidden in God, from what source do your draw your strength . . . your wisdom . . . your motivation?

Christ came not to do His own will, but the will of God who sent Him. He did nothing of Himself, but spoke those things the Father taught Him (John 6:38, 8:28).

Is this true of you? Is your life hidden *with Christ* in God?

In today's reading, notice how Paul entered into this new life and what it cost Him to obey God.

BIBLE READING   *Acts 22*
MEMORY VERSE   *Colossians 3:3*

"It is of the Lord's mercies that we are not consumed, because his compassions fail not."

Lamentations 3:22 (KJ)

HOW MANY times, as nurses, we have felt a deep pity as we cared for a seriously ill or terribly crippled patient. We have stood helpless, wishing for power to heal the hopeless.

On such occasions, there is peace in knowing a Savior whose "compassions fail not." "When he saw the multitudes, he was moved with compassion." "I have compassion on the multitude," said the Lord Jesus, or, in another translation, "My heart aches for the people."

In Christ there is enough compassion to comfort every needy heart.

Pray today that Christian nurses may have wisdom and skill and a special word of comfort for their patients. Pray that those with such tragic need of the Lord Jesus may find Him through the ministry of Christian nurses.

BIBLE READING   *Acts 23*
MEMORY VERSE   *Lamentations 3:22*

FEBRUARY 24

"Whatever your task, work heartily, as serving the Lord and not men."

Colossians 3:23

Do IT as unto the Lord! The hard jobs, the menial tasks, the routine work of nursing . . . can we do these for Him?

See how many things in your nursing day remind you of Him. A blood transfusion . . . the blood of the Lord Jesus is life-giving. A bath . . . remember how He washed His disciples' feet? Death . . . "to me to live is Christ, and to die is gain!" Birth . . . "you must be born anew!" Diet trays . . . Jesus said, "I am the bread of life." A drink of water . . . "the water that I shall give him," said the Lord Jesus, "will become in him a spring of water welling up to eternal life." Tears . . . He shall wipe them away some day. Pain . . . in heaven there shall be no more pain (Revelation 21:4).

Let everything you do today be your gift to Him, because you love Him.

BIBLE READING *Acts 24*
MEMORY VERSE *Colossians 3:23*

FEBRUARY 25

"Moreover it is required of stewards that they be found faithful."

I Corinthians 4:2

I KNOW a nurse who has this motto hanging on her wall and in her heart. It is just two words: "Found Faithful!"

Did you ever notice that the Lord Jesus did not praise the servant for his success or talents or renown, but only for being "good and faithful"? (Matthew 25:21). Could He apply these to you, a Christian nurse?

Faithfulness means doing the things that no one will know about if you leave them undone. Faithfulness means doing the task someone else has neglected (and not grumbling about it). What more are you doing than others? Faithfulness may mean that another nurse will get the credit or will call you "too conscientious."

But God promises that the nurse who is "found faithful" will hear her Lord's "well done."

BIBLE READING   *Acts 25*
MEMORY VERSE   *I Corinthians 4:2*

FEBRUARY 26

"Finally, brethren, farewell. Mend your ways, heed my appeal, agree with one another, live in peace, and the God of love and peace will be with you."

II Corinthians 13:11

"LIVE IN PEACE!"

Every nurse knows that a restful environment is one thing that contributes toward a patient's recovery. And for a healthy Christian life we need the peace of God's presence as our spiritual environment.

"The God of love and peace will be with you." Think of all that such an environment means. We "sit with him in the heavenly places in Christ Jesus." We "seek the things that are above." Our "life is hid with Christ in God." Our "citizenship is in heaven."

Remember to live today as one whose environment is ruled by "the God of love and peace."

BIBLE READING   *Acts 26*
MEMORY VERSE   *II Corinthians 13:11*

FEBRUARY 27

"And let the peace of Christ rule in your hearts, to which indeed you were called in the one body. And be thankful."

Colossians 3:15

FAMILY WORRIES may impede a patient's progress toward health because he may be unable to relax. Such a patient is difficult to help unless the nurse is able to lessen the home problem in some way.

Freedom from worry makes for healthier Christian living, too.

Non-Christian parents? A sick brother? Financial problems? You can leave all your family worries with the Physician in charge of your case, Christian nurse. He is the only One who really understands the problem and has power to do something about it.

When the peace of God rules your heart, worry will be banished as a subversive element. God loves your loved ones more than you do, and He alone knows what is best for them. Trust Him to take care of them for you; thank Him for His sovereignty and faithfulness.

BIBLE READING   *Acts 27*
MEMORY VERSE   *Colossians 3:15*

FEBRUARY 28

"And he came and took her by the hand and lifted her up . . . ." ". . . my glory, and the lifter of my head . . ." ". . . yea, thou liftest me up . . . ."

Mark 1:31; Psalm 3:3, 18:48 (kj)

ARE THINGS "getting you down?"

Christians need not be downcast, for they know One with uplifting power. Let Him lift you up, above the difficulties and temptations of your nursing day, above the sins and failures and sorrows of your tired heart.

If you are not a Christian, then you must come to the Lord Jesus to be lifted up from your sin and helplessness. The Lord Jesus was lifted up on the cross to die for you. "And I, when I am lifted up," He said, "will draw all men to myself." Let Him lift you up into salvation today.

There is no room for downheartedness when your heart is filled with the love of the Lord Jesus. Even circumstances won't "get you down" if you let Him lift your heart above them.

BIBLE READING   *Acts 28*
REVIEW MEMORY VERSE

"Behold, I stand at the door and knock; if any one hears my voice and opens the door, I will come in to him and eat with him, and he with me."

Revelation 3:20

Long though the nurses' day
All through its changing way
Christ moves alone, denied,
Pierced, His side.
Helping the needy sick
Gentle their hands, and quick;
Christ for the nurses stands . . .
Wounded, His hands.
Walking the weary floor,
Tired or depressed, ignored,
Suddenly, Christ they meet . . .
Wounded, His feet.
Problems that nurses fear
Only His Mind can clear.
Christ calleth nurses now . . .
Thorn-crowned, His brow.
Nurses work wearily.
They have no time to see
Christ . . . how the tear-drops start!
Wounded, His heart.

BIBLE READING   *Proverbs 3*
MEMORY VERSE   *Revelation 3:20*

MARCH 1

"And the peace of God, which passes all understanding, will keep your hearts and your minds in Christ Jesus . . . and the God of peace will be with you."

Philippians 4:7, 9

THE peace of God is controlling my heart,
Whatever my circumstance is,
For the God of peace has set me apart,
And my nursing day is His.

The peace of God is a gift of love,
A kindly gift, and sweet,
For the God of peace left His Home above
To make the gift complete.

The peace of God calms my wearied soul,
And the rest I need I see
In the God of peace; while the ages roll
He is calling, "Come to Me."

The peace of God rules over my life,
And lights each pathway dim.
In the God of peace is no room for strife
And I make my home in Him.

BIBLE READING   *Psalms 113, 114*
MEMORY VERSE   *Philippians 4:7*

The Great Physician has an Order Book, and a Christian nurse should be daily studying His orders. Today read the first chapter of the book of Romans in His Order Book, the Bible.

WHAT DOES Romans 1 say about obedience? power? peace?
Read verse 9. How does Paul say he serves?

There are three things Paul says about himself in verses 14, 15 and 16 which should also be true of us as Christian nurses. Substitute the name of your hospital for "Rome," and the kinds of patients for whom you are caring for "Greeks," "Barbarians" and "Jews."

Read verse 18. Why is the wrath of God revealed?

What is sin in God's sight? What may be known about God by everyone? Why did God "give man up?"

BIBLE READING *Romans 1*
MEMORY VERSE *Romans 1:16*

"First, I thank my God through Jesus Christ for all of you, because your faith is proclaimed in all the world. For God is my witness, whom I serve with my spirit in the gospel of his Son, that without ceasing I mention you always in my prayers."

Romans 1:8, 9

THINK of Christian nurses all over the world today, and thank God through Jesus Christ for all of them. How is your faith, as a Christian nurse, spoken of? Pray and trust the Lord Jesus in your daily life so that your world (your hospital, your college residence, your home, your patients) will know that you believe in Him.

As you pray, remember some of the requests you have almost forgotten because God did not answer you immediately.

Pray for specific individuals. Perhaps there is a patient for whom no one else has ever prayed. Maybe God will use you to help to answer your prayer for that one!

As you pray, trust God to answer you.

BIBLE READING *Psalms 115, 116*
MEMORY VERSES *Romans 1:8, 9*

MARCH 4

Read Romans 2 today.

HAVE you noticed that the things we dislike in others are likely to be our own faults. What does the Bible say about this?

What does the 4th verse say about repentance?

Read verse 8. Is obedience important?

What does verse 10 say about peace?

There is a solemn warning given in this chapter to those who are teaching what they do not practice. What is it?

Look at verse 29; if you do the right thing, is the spirit in which you do it important?

What conclusions can you draw with regard to the praise of your friends *vs.* the approval of God?

From this passage, what should be your attitude toward your work today?

BIBLE READING   *Romans 2*
MEMORY VERSE   *Romans 2:11*

MARCH 5

"Peace I leave with you; my peace I give to you; not as the world gives do I give to you. Let not your hearts be troubled, neither let them be afraid."

John 14:27

THE LORD JESUS drew a sharp distinction between those who were of "the world" and those who were "His own." The world is at enmity with God. It was the world that crucified the Lord Jesus. The world therefore cannot give real or lasting peace; it is on the losing side of the battle against sin.

Only the peace of the Lord Jesus Christ can be real and lasting. Only the peace of knowing your sins forgiven, washed away by the blood of His cross, can quiet your troubled heart.

There is only one way to God . . . the Lord Jesus Christ. There is only one way to peace . . . knowing Him.

BIBLE READING   *Psalms 117, 118*
MEMORY VERSE   *John 14:27*

"Now may the God of peace who brought again from the dead our Lord Jesus, the great shepherd of the sheep, by the blood of the eternal covenant, equip you with everything good that you may do his will, working in you that which is pleasing in his sight, through Jesus Christ; to whom be glory for ever and ever. Amen."

Hebrews 13:20, 21

NOTICE that it is the God of peace who is to equip you perfectly. Sin and worry disturb our peace; forgiveness through the blood of the Lord Jesus brings us peace.

When all the world is troubled, the God of peace gives His peace to the trusting heart. The Lord Jesus said, "Peace, be still!" to the stormy sea, and there was a great calm.

Do you know that kind of calm in your heart today? You can know it by trusting the Lord Jesus, who died for you. Bring Him your sin and your failure and your doubt. Let Him cleanse you with His blood and make you His child.

"Therefore, since we are justified by faith, we have peace with God through our Lord Jesus Christ."

BIBLE READING   *Psalm 119:1-16*
MEMORY VERSE   *Hebrews 13:20, 21*

"I am the Lord your God from the land of Egypt; you shall know no God but me, and besides me there is no savior."

Hosea 13:4

A PATIENT who has complete confidence in his doctor has a better chance of recovery than one who does not trust his physician. Some apprehensive patients even return from surgery still struggling to control their anxiety. Fear can cause real difficulty.

Only one Physician knows enough to handle your life. Only one Physician is competent to deal with the problem of your heart. Only one Physician has dealt with the problem of sin and solved it for all time.

You can trust Him with your problems. Let Him have control of your life today.

BIBLE READING   *Psalm 119:17-32*
REVIEW MEMORY VERSES

MARCH 8

"As it is written: 'None is righteous, no, not one.' "

Romans 3:10

EVERYONE has a standard of right and wrong, yet not one of us lives up to that standard. God's standard of perfection is infinitely above ours, so that as far as He is concerned none of us is righteous, not one of us is fit for His holy presence.

You may be a good student nurse, but until you have met the requirements for graduation and state boards, you are not good enough to be an R.N. Goodness is fine, but it doesn't go far enough.

You may be a moral, upright person but that is not enough to get you to heaven.

That is why Jesus died. He loved this world of lost sinners. He saw that we could never measure up to God's standard of holiness So He came to die for our sins and to be made "unto us the righteousness of God." He is the only way to holiness; He is the only way to God.

Read Romans 3 and 4 today. In these chapters God gives us the symptoms, diagnosis, prognosis and specific remedy for the disease of sin. Look for these as you study.

BIBLE READING   *Romans 3, 4*
MEMORY VERSE   *Romans 3:10*

MARCH 9

"Therefore, since we are justified by faith, we have peace with God through our Lord Jesus Christ."

Romans 5:1

WHEN THE EGO is torn by conflicting tensions and frustrations there may be mental illness. Spiritually, there may be tensions, too.

The Christian personality is called "the new man," which is the life of Christ in the believer. "The old man," the sinful personality, still seeks to assert itself. The Christian is to be ruled by Christ, not by the sinful personality any longer. When the Christian is undecided about which shall rule in his life, there may be spiritual illness.

Good spiritual health requires a yielding to the authority of the Lord Jesus in every area where we are in conflict. Spend time with Him. Let Him help you to say "no" to self and "yes" to Him in the situations you will meet today. Who is ruling your life?

BIBLE READING   *Romans 5*
MEMORY VERSE   *Romans 5:1*

MARCH 10

"Do not yield your members to sin as instruments of wickedness, but yield yourselves to God, as men who have been brought from death to life, and your members to God as instruments of righteousness."

Romans 6:13

STUDY Romans 6 today . . . "Sin must not rule!"

In order that Christ may rule in our lives, we who belong to Him are to consider ourselves as dead. As you study this chapter, claim the ruling power of the Lord Jesus for those areas in your life where sin has been ruling.

Pray today for your testimony in the hospital where you work. Pray for the people with whom you work who are not doctors or nurses. Pray that you may be an instrument "of righteousness" to bring healing to sick souls today.

Study verse 13 in the light of what you know about instruments. Can you apply this knowledge to your usefulness as a Christian instrument?

BIBLE READING   *Romans 6*
MEMORY VERSE   *Romans 6:13*

MARCH 11

Romans 7 is the study for today. It is the story of the struggle between the old, sinful personality and the new personality where Christ rules. Which is victorious?

> O FOR A closer walk with God,
> A calm and heavenly frame,
> A light to shine upon the road
> That leads me to the Lamb!
> The dearest idol I have known,
> Whate'er that idol be,
> Help me to tear it from Thy throne
> And worship only Thee.
> So shall my walk be close with God,
> Calm and serene my frame;
> So purer light shall mark the road
> That leads me to the Lamb.
>
> William Cowper

BIBLE READING *Romans 7*
MEMORY VERSE *Romans 5:8*

MARCH 12

"Likewise the Spirit helps us in our weakness; for we do not know how to pray as we ought, but the Spirit himself intercedes for us with sighs too deep for words. And he who searches the hearts of men knows what is the mind of the Spirit, because the Spirit intercedes for the saints according to the will of God."

Romans 8:26, 27

REMEMBER as you pray today that prayer in the Spirit is always "according to the will of God." Test your prayers by this rule. Only the Holy Spirit of God can teach you to pray.

Can you truthfully say with the Lord Jesus, "Nevertheless, not my will, but Thine be done?"

Ask God to search your heart and show you anything there which is not according to His will. Then give yourself to Him for cleansing.

Now read I John 5:14 and 15.

BIBLE READING *Psalms 120, 121*
MEMORY VERSE *Romans 8:26, 27*

"And we know that all things work together for good to them that love God, to them who are the called according to his purpose."

Romans 8:28 (KJ)

HAVE YOU EVER visited the laboratory of the love of God? He is testing and trying and examining our lives, trying to bring us to healthy maturity in Him.

Sometimes He uses very complicated tests which we do not understand at all. Sometimes He takes a long time with His testing and sometimes the tests are short. But He is the One who gives the orders, and it's important to remember that His orders are rooted in His love for you.

Look at your difficulties today through the microscope of God's love. See how the meaning of each trouble is always "working together for good" because you are "called according to his purpose."

Some of the tests in His laboratory are painful. But He understands that too and even as He draws the blood He tells you, "This won't last long, and it is for your good."

"See what love the Father has given us, that we should be called children of God . . . ."

BIBLE READING   *Psalms 122, 123*
MEMORY VERSE   *Romans 8:28*

"All these things are against me."

Genesis 42:36 (KJ)

JUST WHEN God was about to work out something wonderful, Jacob began complaining. "All these things," he said mournfully, counting his troubles instead of his blessings, "are against me."

Do you ever feel like that? Everything went wrong today, we say, just everything! Things couldn't be worse!

God's Word says, "All things work together for good to them that love God, to them who are the called according to his purpose."

Read Romans 8:37, 11:36; I Corinthians 3:21 and 16:14.

Everything wrong? All things against you? "I will bless the Lord at all times; his praise shall continually be in my mouth."

BIBLE READING *Psalms 124, 125*
REVIEW MEMORY VERSES

MARCH 15

"He who did not spare his own Son, but gave him up for us all, will he not also give us all things with him?"

Romans 8:32

PRAY FOR Christian nurses all over the world who are meeting together for prayer and Bible study and seeking to win other nurses to the Lord Jesus. Pray that each one will be given a spirit of love for the others in the group so that the Lord's work will not be hindered. Pray that small groups will be encouraged to be faithful and that large groups will not grow cold.

Then pray for your own hospital. Is there a group of nurses there who meet for prayer and Bible study? If not, pray that you may be used to bring others to know the Lord Jesus and to want to study His Word.

We need each other for growth and encouragement and for a united testimony. Ask God to show you your part in making Christ known in your hospital.

BIBLE READING   *Psalms 126, 127*
MEMORY VERSE   *Romans 8:32*

MARCH 16

"We were buried therefore with him by baptism into death, so that as Christ was raised from the dead by the glory of the Father, we too might walk in newness of life."

Romans 6:4

THE SAME wonderful power that raised the Lord Jesus Christ from the dead is the power that enables us to live our new lives in Him.

As you study Romans 8 today, look for all that is said about the Holy Spirit. What part does He play in your new life as a believer?

Look at verse 28. Define "all things" as it applies to your life today.

Read verse 32. What is included under "all things" in this context?

Think through verse 37. What does "all things" mean here? What do you think it means to be "more than conquerors?"

What can separate you from the love of God in Christ?

BIBLE READING   *Romans 8*
MEMORY VERSE   *Romans 6:4*

MARCH 17

"To set the mind on the flesh is death, but to set the mind on the Spirit is life and peace."

Romans 8:6

WHEN THE SPIRIT of God is ruling there is real peace, not just a temporary truce. Being spiritually minded means that our attitudes will be like Christ's attitudes. It means that the things we think about will be worthwhile things. It means that we will resolutely set our minds against thoughts that are wrong, or not of Him. The Bible talks about "bringing into captivity every thought to the obedience of Christ."

When Christ rules, He rules absolutely or He does not rule at all.

Is He ruling in your life today?

BIBLE READING   *Psalms 128, 129*
MEMORY VERSE   *Romans 8:6*

MARCH 18

"Behold like the clay in the potter's hand, so are you in my hand . . . ."
Jeremiah 18:6

I AM but a little vessel, like the cruse of oil in Scripture,
Yet who knows what prophet's passing by my way?
And though little I'm possessing,
Christ through me may souls be blessing;
He will keep my empty vessel full of grace for every day.

Make me like the empty vessels at the Galilean wedding,
At the wedding where the Savior was a guest;
May I, filled to overflowing
With the peace of simply knowing,
By the sweet Word of the Savior, put some other guest to rest.

I am but an empty vessel, just a pitcher, to be broken
'Til the light that is the Savior's shines to all;
As Your servant, Savior, take me
And to Your own honor break me.
Let Your light shine out by breaking, help some other heed Your call.

BIBLE READING   *Romans 9*
MEMORY VERSE   *Romans 8:37*

MARCH 19

"So then faith cometh by hearing, and hearing by the word of God."
Romans 10:17 (KJ)

SOMETIMES we wish we had more faith, forgetting that listening to God's Word is a sure way of increasing our faith. Do you want to be strong in faith? Then spend much time with the Word of God.

The more you learn about God through His Book, the more your faith will grow.

Of course you may not know that you have great faith. You will be thinking about what a faithful God you have. You may even be convicted of your lack of faith. But others will know. And He whom you most want to please will know it too.

BIBLE READING   *Psalms 130, 131*
MEMORY VERSE   *Romans 10:17*

MARCH 20

"Brethren, my heart's desire and prayer to God for them is that they might be saved."

Romans 10:1

ROMANS 10 is a missionary chapter. It was because of this kind of praying that Paul could be the kind of preacher he was. As you study this chapter, ask God to put in your heart genuine concern for your friends who don't know Him. Be specific.

Pray for Christian nurses on the mission field. Many times their time for prayer and Bible study is limited because of the pressure of their work. Pray that they may make the very best use of the time they have and that they may be kept in a spirit of prayer as they serve.

Perhaps God wants you to go and help them. Pray that He will make His will known to you. Pray also that as He does, you will be willing to do it.

BIBLE READING   *Romans 10*
MEMORY VERSE   *Romans 8:38, 39*

MARCH 21

"For from him and through him and to him are all things: To him be glory for ever. Amen."

Romans 11:36

As YOU STUDY Romans 11 today, remember that the first missionaries were Jewish Christians who brought the gospel to the Gentiles. If it had not been for the Jews, we might never have known Christ.

Examine your attitudes toward the Jewish people. Are they consistent with God's attitude toward them? Remember that Jesus Christ was a Jew. What about your feelings toward other minority groups? Read verse 32.

Read verse 36. What things in your life are yours through Jesus Christ? What things in your life can you return to Him again by the use you make of them? By your Christian service? By your thankfulness?

Begin now to let all that you have and are bring glory to Him.

BIBLE READING   *Romans 11*
MEMORY VERSE   *Romans 11:36*

MARCH 22

"I appeal to you therefore, brethren, by the mercies of God, to present your bodies as a living sacrifice, holy and acceptable to God, which is your spiritual worship. Do not be conformed to this world but be transformed by the renewal of your mind, that you may prove what is the will of God, what is good and acceptable and perfect."

Romans 12:1, 2

NOW THAT I am a Christian, what about my amusements? What about my friends? Are there certain things Christian nurses cannot do, or places where they shouldn't go?

When you are with your patients there are restrictions which you realize are necessary for maximum efficiency. There are rules for the safety of the patient, and rules about the appearance of the nurse which are for the good of the profession as a whole.

Even at home or on dates the behavior of a nurse can reflect on others in the profession. "Nurses are hard," people say. Or, "You are like a nurse, so gentle . . ." No one should generalize about a group from the behavior of a few, but most people do.

Christian nurses must consider their behavior, too, in the light of maximum efficiency in accomplishing their service for God. What are His purposes for you today? What will best help you do His will or represent His family to others?

BIBLE READING   *Psalms 132, 133*
MEMORY VERSES   *Romans 12:1, 2*

". . . he who does acts of mercy, with cheerfulness."

Romans 12:8

THE FIRST verse of Romans 12 tells you what to do; the rest of the chapter tells you something about how to "present your body a living sacrifice."

As you read, notice how important differences are. Some nurses are clever with their hands, while others have skill with organization. Some are good with emergencies, while some have particular tenderness for the geriatric patient. Some nurses are handy in surgery; others like maternity or pediatrics. Isn't it a good thing we aren't all interested in the same type of nursing?

That's the way it is in the family of God. You have certain characteristics that no one else ever has had or ever will have. You are the only one who can do the task He has planned for you today.

Present yourself now to Him for His use.

BIBLE READING   *Romans 12*
REVIEW MEMORY VERSES

"But put on the Lord Jesus Christ, and make no provision for the flesh, to gratify its desires."

Romans 13:14

READ ROMANS 13 today. This is a short chapter, but full of practical advice for Christian nurses.

What does it say about obedience? Do you think it is all right for Christians to break college or hospital rules? Why, or why not?

What is our standing debt to others?

What does this chapter say about honesty?

What do you think this chapter would teach us about "gripe" sessions and petty quarreling?

What do you think it means to "make provision for the flesh?"

What is the "armor of light?"

BIBLE READING   *Romans 13*
MEMORY VERSE   *Romans 13:14*

MARCH 25

"If we live, we live to the Lord, and if we die, we die to the Lord; so then, whether we live or whether we die, we are the Lord's."

Romans 14:8

A MAN who had been a bitterly complaining patient was completely transformed when he accepted the Lord Jesus. A Christian nurse was used to lead him to the Lord. He had never heard the gospel before he came into the hospital. He lived his new joy for exactly a week; he died following surgery.

> Lord Jesus, I thank You I live,
> for a man today died,
> having known Your victory
> only a week.
> Seven short days to feel Your uplifting power
> renewing his strength;
> Six nights to seek and find Your hand
> in the dark.
> ("There is no night there . . .")
> A week of trusting and tears;
> then his faith was sight . . .
> In strife seven days . . . O my Captain . . .
> Thanks for the warfare of life!

BIBLE READING *Psalms 134, 135*
MEMORY VERSE *Romans 14:8*

MARCH 26

"So each of us shall give account of himself to God. Then let us no more pass judgment on one another, but rather decide never to put a stumbling block or hindrance in the way of a brother."

Romans 14:12, 13

WE CAN LISTEN to sermons or read the Word of God in such a way that we miss the important part of the lesson. "I hope Jane reads this . . . or hears that . . ." we think. "My, this is just what Bob needs!"

Bible study should bring a very personal blessing. Until we see the Lord Jesus and become fully like Him, there will always be something He will want to change in our lives.

Look for the stumbling blocks in your life which may be in your brother's (or sister's) way. Ask the Lord to make you willing and help you to move them.

BIBLE READING   *Psalms 136, 137*
MEMORY VERSE   *Romans 14:12, 13*

MARCH 27

"We are the Lord's."

Romans 14:8

NURSES have an insight into the private lives of individuals that few others have. This can give us a great deal of tolerance and understanding, or it can make us carping critics of the other person's weaknesses.

As you study Romans 14 today, study also your own attitudes in the light of these verses.

Pray for your patients today and for their visitors.

Pray that you may have understanding in dealing with these visitors. And determine that with God's help you will "live unto the Lord" in all that you do today.

BIBLE READING   *Romans 14*
MEMORY VERSE   *Romans 10:9, 10*

MARCH 28

"Who are you to pass judgment on the servant of another? It is before his own master that he stands or falls. And he will be upheld, for the Master is able to make him stand."

Romans 14:4

> GOD give us hearts to understand our brother,
> Lips that speak in love of one another.
> Seeing earthly ways, open our eyes
> And make us very slow to criticize.

Lord, we have nothing we have not received;
How often must Your tender heart have grieved
To see our pride and arrogance and hate.
We judge. We see his good things far too late
And only grieve for what we've done or said
When we are scolded, or the man is dead.
Guard our lips. In speaking of each other
Give us a gentle love for one another.

BIBLE READING   *Psalms 138, 139*
MEMORY VERSE   *Romans 14:4*

MARCH 29

"For Christ did not please himself; but, as it is written, 'The reproaches of those who reproached thee fell on me.'"

Romans 15:3

THE STUDY of Romans 15 will give you some interesting answers to these questions:

Can a strong Christian live for himself without regard for others and their needs?

Do you have responsibilities toward weaker Christians in your place of service today? What are they?

How can you be filled with all joy and peace?

What are the missionary verses of this chapter?

How did Paul ask the Christians at Rome to pray?

What is the connection between "joy" and "the will of God"?

There are three verses which tell you something special about God in this chapter. He is a God of patience and consolation, a God of hope, and a God of peace. He is just the God to meet every need of yours!

BIBLE READING   *Romans 15*
MEMORY VERSE   *Romans 15:3*

"For while your obedience is known to all, so that I rejoice over you, I would have you wise as to what is good, and guileless as to what is evil."

Romans 16:19

REREAD Romans 1:8. In the first chapter of Romans Paul commends the Christians for their faith; in the last chapter, which you are studying today, he commends them for their obedience. Faith and obedience go together for a good testimony to the world.

Study the Christians in Romans 16. Can others say of you that you are a "helper in the Lord"? Are you a "worker in the Lord," like Tryphena and Tryphosa, or do you "work hard in the Lord" like the beloved Persis? Be sure that nothing in your life is causing division among Christians, like those mentioned in verse 17.

Verse 27 mentions "the only wise God." What does James 1:5 say about Him?

BIBLE READING *Romans 16*
REVIEW MEMORY VERSES

"Do your best to present yourself to God as one approved, a workman who has no need to be ashamed, rightly handling the word of truth."

II Timothy 2:15

THIS month you have studied the entire book of Romans. Today would be a good day to review what you have learned. You might put a title to each paragraph or chapter of the book. Maybe you would like to choose a verse from each chapter which particularly interests you. Perhaps you could study the ways in which the Lord Jesus is shown in this book to be enough for your personal needs.

Pray that the lessons you have learned may be practical in your every day living. Remember that a skill to be learned must be practiced.

BIBLE READING *Psalms 140, 141*
MEMORY VERSE *II Timothy 2:15*

APRIL 1

"For God is at work in you, both to will and to work for his good pleasure."
Philippians 2:13

ARE you tired of the tangles wrought
By other Christians' quirks?
Try love; it works!
Are you frightened of the danger
That at every corner lurks?
Try trust; it works!
Are you wearied of your labors
While the other fellow shirks?
Try hope; it works!
Would you like to reach the heathen,
Hindus, Africans, and Turks?
Try prayer; it works!
Is your life a peck o'trouble
That disturbs and pains and irks?
Try faith; it works!
Is your happiness so changeable
That it comes and goes in jerks?
Try joy; it works!
Are your efforts met with jeering,
Scoffing, ridicule and smirks?
Try grace; it works!

BIBLE READING   *I Corinthians 1*
MEMORY VERSE   *Philippians 2:13*

"The Lord sustains him on his sickbed; thou wilt make all his bed in his sickness. I said, Lord, be merciful unto me; heal my soul; for I have sinned against thee."

Psalm 41:3, 4 (KJ)

A COMFORTABLE bed is firm and smooth. It has a good foundation. It has clean fresh linen, and the corners of a well-made bed are neat.

For our soul's foundation, God gives us healing peace through Jesus Christ. He gives us forgiveness of sins and cleansing by the water of the Word. We can rest our souls upon His promises. Our Lord knows how to smooth and strengthen the corners of our lives.

If you make beds today, think of Him.

BIBLE READING   *I Corinthians 2*
MEMORY VERSE   *Psalm 41:3, 4*

"Now there are varieties of gifts, but the same Spirit; and there are varieties of service, but the same Lord; and there are diversities of working, but it is the same God who inspires them all in every one. To each is given the manifestation of the Spirit for the common good."

I Corinthians 12:4-7

THINK OF ALL the instruments needed in surgery to perform one minor operation. Each has its particular use and every one is necessary. Suppose the small mosquito forceps refused to be used because it was not a gleaming retractor, or a Kelly forceps felt useless because it was not a tonsil snare!

In God's work, too, each of us is needed in a place of His planning. We each have a special work to do, like no one else's work in all the world.

Give yourself to Him, then, so that the Holy Spirit of God may use you to manifest Jesus Christ to those who need Him.

BIBLE READING   *I Corinthians 3*
MEMORY VERSE   *I Corinthians 12:4-7*

APRIL 4

"These were the potters, and those that dwelt among plants and hedges: there they dwelt with the king for his work."

I Chronicles 4:23 (KJ)

THERE ARE RESTRICTIONS in the life of all nurses. They are often on duty when they would rather be out on a date. They may not say the hasty word, may not cry when they are deeply troubled, may not even show by the expression on their faces what their feelings are.

Sometimes we are restricted until we feel, with Job, like those "whom God has hedged in."

Let's study hedges today!

There's a protecting hedge in Job 1:10. There's a hedge of restriction in Lamentations 3:7. Paul's attitude toward his personal hedge is given in II Corinthians 4:8-11. There's a hedge for missionaries in Luke 14:23 (and also in Ezekiel 22:30).

No matter how dull and routine our nursing days may become, however "hedged in" we may be, we still may be like the potters who "dwelt with the king for his work."

BIBLE READING   *I Corinthians 4*
REVIEW MEMORY VERSES

APRIL 5

"Through him then let us continually offer up the sacrifice of praise to God, that is, the fruit of lips that acknowledge his name."

Hebrews 13:15

TAKE TIME today to praise God for all the good things He has given you. What answers to prayer have you had this year?

List the things you have which God might take away. Praise Him for the little things that make you happy. Praise Him for the great gift of life itself with all its opportunities for love and laughter and joy.

Thank Him today for health and for all the privileges of being a nurse. Thank Him for the Lord Jesus and for His death on the cross for you.

Praise God for other Christian nurses and ask Him to use you to bring other nurses to Him today.

Praise God with joy today. True joy is God's prophylaxis for unbelief.

BIBLE READING   *I Corinthians 5*
MEMORY VERSE   *Hebrews 13:15*

APRIL 6

"Is anything too hard for the Lord?"

Genesis 18:14

YOUR ANSWER to this question makes all the difference between defeated and victorious Christian living. Is it too hard for Him to make you what you ought to be? Is it too hard for Him to give you faith or strength or joy or courage? Is it too hard for Him to make you a witness in your hospital situation or wherever you may be?

Acknowledge your dependence on God today. He is at work within you. He can do what you cannot do. Consult Him with your doubts and problems. Let Him do what is too hard for you.

Read the question again. Answer it honestly.

BIBLE READING   *I Corinthians 6*
MEMORY VERSE   *Genesis 18:14*

"No temptation has overtaken you that is not common to man. God is faithful, and he will not let you be tempted beyond your strength, but with the temptation will also provide the way of escape, that you may be able to endure it."
"For the moment all discipline seems painful rather than pleasant; later it yields the peaceful fruit of righteousness to those who have been trained by it . . . for our God is a consuming fire."

I Corinthians 10:13; Hebrews 12:11, 29

A USEFUL instrument must be subjected to an uncomfortable degree of heat. So God is called a "consuming fire," burning away the organisms of sin which make us useless in His service.

Let the hard things that you meet today, the disappointments, the griefs, the little irritations and the nagging heartaches be His ways of making you clean for His use. Look for the "way of escape" with each temptation, so that afterwards you may know that even these things have drawn you closer to your Lord.

No trouble can outweigh the blessing that goes with it.

BIBLE READING *I Corinthians 7*
MEMORY VERSE *I Corinthians 10:13*

"We destroy arguments, and every proud obstacle to the knowledge of God, and take every thought captive to obey Christ."

II Corinthians 10:5

IN THE BATTLES of the Christian life, you are either the "prisoner of war" of your thoughts or your thoughts are prisoners of Christ. There is no freedom apart from devotion to Him.

Take every thought today and let it be His captive. The thoughts of your work . . . let them serve Him who can make you a cheerful worker, accurate and faithful in the least detail of nursing care. Thoughts of your leisure . . . let them serve Him who can give real relaxation and prepare you for better service in the future. Thoughts of things to come . . . let them serve Him by refusing every worry and trusting Him who owns you to make your way perfect. Thoughts of non-Christian loved ones . . . let them serve Him, bringing you into His presence in prayer.

Take every thought captive. Let each one be a thought of obedience to your Captor, Christ.

BIBLE READING   *I Corinthians 8*
MEMORY VERSE   *II Corinthians 10:5*

APRIL 9

"Bear one another's burdens, and so fulfil the law of Christ. . . . So then, as we have opportunity, let us do good to all men, and especially to those who are of the household of faith."

Galatians 6:2, 10

BEARING the burden of prayer for others provides an opportunity for you to "do good to all men."

Wait quietly before the Lord today and ask Him to give you a burden for those who need your prayers. Then ask Him to show you ways in which you can help them by other methods too.

Are there letters you could write which might help someone who needs Him? Is there something you can say for Him today? Perhaps you can show by a cheerful attitude about your work that the people who know our God are happy.

Spend time in prayer and in service today.

BIBLE READING   *I Corinthians 9*
MEMORY VERSE   *Galatians 6:2*

APRIL 10

"If my people who are called by my name humble themselves, and pray and seek my face, and turn from their wicked ways, then will I hear from heaven, and will forgive their sin and heal their land."

II Chronicles 7:14

MANY OF US are praying for revival, but what we mean is revival for the other fellow! It's easy to pray for God's awakening to come to others; it's hard to humble ourselves and ask God to show us our own wicked ways. And having seen our sin, it is easier to keep on praying for forgiveness than it is to turn resolutely from that thing in our lives which is hindering God's work in us and through us.

Let's put away our excuses and turn to God ourselves, with every personal sin put away. Let's remind ourselves — "Revival . . . always . . . begins with *me*!"

UMBRELLAS

God showers blessing down.
Some day
I think we may regret
Steel-ribbed excuses we've put up
Lest our vain pride
Get wet . . .

BIBLE READING   *I Corinthians 10*
MEMORY VERSE   *II Chronicles 7:14*

APRIL 11

"Jesus . . . rose from supper, laid aside his garments, and girded himself with a towel. Then he poured water into a basin, and began to wash the disciples' feet, and to wipe them with the towel with which he was girded." " . . . but emptied himself, taking the form of a servant being born in the likeness of men. And being found in human form he humbled himself and became obedient unto death, even death on a cross. . . ."

John 13:4, 5, Philippians 2:7, 8

IN YOUR ROUTINE work today you may be taking a towel and pouring water into a basin and washing patient's feet. The humdrum tasks of nursing were not above our Lord. It makes the hard things easier, to know He understands all about them, and it makes us humble too to think of the Lord of lords and King of kings washing His disciples' feet.

He became a man like other men so that you might see His example, the example of the sinless Son of God, obedient unto death.

He washed His disciples' feet. What task is beneath us as we serve others for love of Him?

BIBLE READING   *I Corinthians 11*
MEMORY VERSE   *Philippians 2:7, 8*

APRIL 12

"Humble yourselves therefore under the mighty hand of God, that in due time he may exalt you. Cast all your anxieties on him, for he cares for you."
I Peter 5:6, 7

ARE YOU HUMBLE enough to cast all your care upon Him, or are you so proud that you must be anxious and worried about things which are His concern, not yours?

Difficulties and cares are your chances to prove your trust in Him. Anxiety and real prayer cannot live in the same heart.

He cares for you. A patient who is under the care of a competent physician does not need to worry about his medicine or his treatment; that's up to the doctor.

You are under the care of the Great Physician. Give Him your life and let Him take your anxiety. He cares for you.

BIBLE READING   *I Corinthians 12*
MEMORY VERSE   *I Peter 5:6, 7*

APRIL 13

"Love bears all things, believes all things, hopes all things, endures all things. . . ."
I Corinthians 13:7

THIS CHAPTER has become so familiar to many of us that we lose the practical meaning behind the beautiful words.

Spend some time trying to write verses 1-7 in your own words. Make it apply to your particular nursing situation.

Perhaps you might begin, "I may speak my professional language cleverly, and know all about different diseases, but if I don't have loving sympathy for my patients, I'm just like someone banging a cymbal, disturbing the quiet of the hospital."

Write the other verses in your own words and then write them carefully on your heart for your day's work.

BIBLE READING *I Corinthians 13*
MEMORY VERSE *I Corinthians 13:7*

APRIL 14

"And when the people complained, it displeased the Lord . . . ."

Numbers 11:1 (KJ)

HAVE YOU EVER been in a nurses' "gripe" session? I have, and I'm afraid I added my complaints just as loudly as the rest. I've been discovering, though, what the Bible has to say about grumbling and complaining, and it makes me ashamed. Let's see what the Bible says about . . .

Complaining about each other? *James* 5:9
Complaining about what you have to give? *II Corinthians* 9:7
Grumbling about visitors? *I Peter* 4:9
Grumbling in the dormitory? *Psalm 106:25*
Complaining about duties? *Philippians 2:14, 15*
Grumbling about meals? *Exodus 16:8*

BIBLE READING *I Corinthians 14*
REVIEW MEMORY VERSES

APRIL 15

"Count it all joy, my brethren ,when you meet various trials. . . ."

James 1:2

"COUNT IT ALL joy . . ." when you meet people who annoy you and irritate you. "Count it all joy . . ." when interruptions intrude even on your quiet time. "Count it all joy . . ." when the patients are cranky and the doctors impatient and no one on your team works as hard as you. "Count it all joy . . ." when everything goes wrong and your money runs out and people complain when you're doing your very best. Yes, "count it all joy. . . ."

How? First, don't pretend that things are different from what they really are, and don't pretend that you are not annoyed when you really feel that way. Face your problem. Look at it clearly. Then bring it to the One who said, "happy is the people, whose God is the Lord" (Psalm 144:15), and trust Him to give you His joy for your irritation and distress.

Why? Because all these things "try your faith" and can be used to make you a stronger, more patient, more mature Christian nurse for the Lord Jesus.

BIBLE READING   *I Corinthians 15*
MEMORY VERSE   *James 1:2*

APRIL 16

"These things I have spoken to you, that my joy might be in you, and that your joy might be full."

John 15:11

HIS JOY . . . for you! "Be of good cheer," the Lord Jesus says to you today, "I have overcome the world."

The joy of the Lord Jesus is a gladness that does not depend on circumstances. His friends forsook Him, but the Father was with Him. He was weary and hungry and the people He loved did not understand Him. He suffered the agony of coming to His own people and His own did not receive Him. Yet He had joy, His own joy, to give away!

As you study this verse, take His joy for your day. Whatever your circumstances, He is with you in them to overcome all difficulties by His power.

He will not only enable you to do the impossible — He will enable you to do it cheerfully!

BIBLE READING   *I Corinthians 16*
MEMORY VERSE   *John 15:11*

APRIL 17

"Who serve unto the example and shadow of heavenly things . . ."

Hebrews 8:5 (KJ)

MANY of the characters in the Old Testament are "types," or pictures of the Lord Jesus Christ. In your Bible study today see how many ways in which you can find similarities to the Lord Jesus in the lives of Joseph and Moses. Read:

Genesis 37:4, 8, 16-18; 39:3; 40:14;
    41:46, 55; 42:8; 45:5, 13, 21, 26
John 1:11; 2:5
Mark 7:37
Luke 3:23;22:19
Hebrews 11:23-28

You may find other pictures for yourself. These shadowy pictures are usually not perfect in every detail, because the Bible is very accurate in showing human weakness, and our Lord Jesus never sinned. But you will find many beautiful similarities in these Old Testament shadows and types.

BIBLE READING *II Corinthians 1*
REVIEW MEMORY VERSES

APRIL 18

". . . so that you may not be sluggish, but imitators of those who through faith and patience inherit the promises."

Hebrews 6:12

CLAIMING God's promises through faith and prayer is no work for lazy souls. It takes steady stick-to-it-ive-ness to be a real follower.

Peter looked around and saw John "following." When other nurses look at you, do they see you following or lagging behind? The Lord Jesus said, "My sheep hear my voice, and I know them, and they follow me . . . ," and "Follow me, and I will make you fishers of men . . . ," and "If any man serve me, let him follow me . . . ."

BIBLE READING   *II Corinthians 2*
MEMORY VERSE   *Hebrews 6:12*

APRIL 19

"Then we which are alive and remain shall be caught up together with them in the clouds, to meet the Lord in the air: and so shall we ever be with the Lord."

I Thessalonians 4:17

SOME DAY the Lord Jesus is coming back to take those who belong to Him to be with Him forever. If you are not His child, you will be left behind.

But you do not need to be left out! Jesus died for you. He took your sins on the cross, and all that is lacking to make you His child is your faith. Will you trust Him, make Him your very own Savior by your faith in Him? Then when He comes, He will take you with Him.

And He will be with you in a very wonderful way as you live your life day by day. His "forever" begins right here!

BIBLE READING   *II Corinthians 3*
MEMORY VERSE   *I Thessalonians 4:17*

APRIL 20

"May you be strengthened with all power, according to his glorious might, for all endurance and patience with joy."

Colossians 1:11

WE USUALLY quote the first half of this verse and forget the last half. We all want to be strong . . . but who wants to be patient and endure with joy? Yet that is just why Paul is praying for strength for these Colossian Christians!

Things weren't always easy for the Colossians. They faced suffering as well as the same minor irritations that you and I chafe under.

It takes a lot of might and power to be patient and longsuffering with joyfulness when everything on the ward goes wrong and every assignment you get is trying and difficult and depressing. Then it's time to ask for His supply of your need . . . "according to His glorious might."

You can be patient and cheerful and longsuffering today . . . according to His glorious might!

BIBLE READING   *II Corinthians 4*
MEMORY VERSE   *Colossians 1:11*

APRIL 21

"His divine power has granted us all things that pertain to life and godliness, through the knowledge of him who called us to his own glory and excellence."

II Peter 1:3

BEGIN by reading II Peter 1:1-8 today. We are given all things that we need for our lives as Christian nurses. We have the exceeding great promises, enough supply to meet every need of ours. Requisitions on God's "central supply" are always filled, and we are always given more than we had thought to ask for too.

List eight characteristics which the Christian is to add to his "all things." How do you measure up in this adding to your faith?

Study verses 3 and 8. What is said about knowing the Lord?

BIBLE READING   *II Corinthians 5*
MEMORY VERSE   *II Peter 1:3*

APRIL 22

"And all the women that were wisehearted did spin with their hands, and brought that which they had spun, both of blue, and of purple, and of scarlet, and of fine linen."

Exodus 35:25 (KJ)

MAKING THE CURTAINS for the Lord's house, the willing-hearted women spun beautiful thread. We are spinning, too, day by day, fibers that will last forever; all the things we do for the Lord make up those threads.

Don't you love blue? The color of the sky, reminding us of the mercy of our Lord, of loyalty, honor, worship and truth for Him who is the Truth and the Life. Have you spun any blue threads today?

And the wisehearted women spun purple threads too — purple, the royal color. In everything we, the King's daughters, do, should be woven the purple threads of His Lordship in our obedient lives.

The scarlet threads are beautiful and very costly, for they speak of sacrifice. Think of God's great sacrifice of His Son and what it means to you today.

Don't forget the fine linen threads of holiness and purity. Read I Peter 1:16 and Titus 2:14.

Spin with a willing heart today!

BIBLE READING   *II Corinthians 6*
REVIEW MEMORY VERSES

APRIL 23

"And all the women whose heart stirred them up in wisdom spun goats' hair."

Exodus 35:26 (KJ)

SOME OF THE WOMEN who were spinning for the Lord's house were more than wisehearted. Their hearts "stirred them up in wisdom." They were particularly concerned, apparently, for the glory of the Lord. Yet notice their spinning . . . just "goats' hair!" Nobody would come to admire the lovely colors of their work. It was strong and sturdy and would make the firm fabric of the tabernacle itself; but don't you think these women sometimes longed to spin the beautiful colors, too?

Much of our work as Christian nurses is like "spinning goats' hair." It's work with our hands on rough fabric, common work, sometimes not at all beautiful. Yet He sees when the rough threads cut our fingers and get tangled and hard to weave and He will use our faith and love and patience in a dwelling for Himself.

And whatever it is we are spinning, Lord, let our hands bring to You the thread of a willing heart.

BIBLE READING   *II Corinthians 7*
REVIEW MEMORY VERSES

APRIL 24

"This is the service of the families of the Gershonites, to serve, and for burdens . . ."

Numbers 4:24 (KJ)

THE GERSHONITES' work wasn't so very different from the work of nurses. The Lord recorded their service and He is remembering yours too. Whatever your service, remember that you are serving Him.

Pray today for nurses who have particularly lonely places of service or especially difficult burdens. Ask the Lord to help them sense His readiness to help. Pray that non-Christian nurses may realize their need of Him.

Perhaps there is someone whose service or burden you should share today by word or letter. Ask God to lead you to that one.

BIBLE READING *II Corinthians 8*
REVIEW MEMORY VERSES

APRIL 25

"The blessing of the Lord makes rich, and he adds no sorrow with it."

Proverbs 10:22

NURSES USUALLY aren't very wealthy. But Christian nurses have riches that will last forever. Today's Bible study will tell you something about your riches.

Revelation 2:9
I Corinthians 1:5
Psalm 104:24
Ephesians 3:8, 1:7, 2:4
I Timothy 6:17, 18
Colossians 2:2, 3; 3:16
Proverbs 10:22
James 2:5

From these passages, you now know something of the extent, kind, and permanence of your riches. What can you do with them?

BIBLE READING *II Corinthians 9*
MEMORY VERSE *Proverbs 10:22*

"'And the Lord said to me, "Behold I have begun to give Sihon and his land over to you; begin to take possession, that you may occupy his land." ... And we captured all his cities . . .; there was not a city too high for us; the Lord our God gave all into our hands.'" "Thus the Lord gave to Israel all the land which he swore to give to their fathers; and having taken possession of it, they settled there. And the Lord gave them rest on every side just as he had sworn to their fathers; not one of all their enemies had withstood them, for the Lord had given all their enemies into their hands."

Deuteronomy 2:31, 34, 36; Joshua 21:43-45

THE STORY of the way God worked in the lives of the Israelites has its counterpart in the way He wants to work in your life today, Christian nurse! When He begins to give, He wants you to begin to possess. When He delivers you, He wants you to have complete victory; no sin, that worst enemy of yours, need be too strong for you; not one! The Lord wants to give you rest . . . real rest . . . rest that doesn't depend on the circumstances of your busy days.

BIBLE READING *II Corinthians 10*
REVIEW MEMORY VERSES

I will stand me upon my watch, and set me upon the tower, and will watch to see what he will say unto me, and what I shall answer when I am reproved."

Habakkuk 2:1 (KJ)

THE WORD OF GOD is profitable for "doctrine, reproof, correction, and instruction in righteousness." As you study and pray, watch to see what the Lord wants to say to you.

Pray for Christian nurses in places of temptation today. Some of them may be neglecting their daily time of quiet with God. Pray that today they may "watch to see what He will say."

Pray too for missionary nurses today. Some of them may be in danger, some of them are in need, some are on furlough. Pray that God will direct their hearts to the love of Him.

Then ask the Lord to bless prospective missionary nurses, that they may not forget to watch and so lose their vision for the field.

Are you listening for His voice?

BIBLE READING   *II Corinthians 11*
MEMORY VERSE   *Habakkuk 2:1*

APRIL 28

"For we are His workmanship . . . ."

Ephesians 2:10

DEAR NURSE, you're His!
And so I'm glad for you,
Glad, for your whole life through
In joy and sorrow too,
You're His.

Dear nurse, you're His.
Held in a mighty hand,
He who the world has planned
Holds your life-pattern grand;
You're His.

Dear nurse, you're His.
He keeps you by His power,
Sends sunshine with each shower,
Stays near you every hour.
You're His.

Dear nurse, you're His.
Savior, Redeemer, Friend,
He loves you to the end.
All you may need He'll send.
You're His.

BIBLE READING   *II Corinthians 12*
MEMORY VERSE   *Ephesians 2:10*

"I have said this to you, that in me you may have peace. In the world you have tribulation; but be of good cheer, I have overcome the world."

John 16:33

NOTICE that it is the Lord's own peace which He leaves with us. His peace . . . what is it like?

His was peace that rested, that first Sabbath day, after He had brought order out of chaos and man from the dust of the earth.

His was the peace of communion, as He walked with Enoch and called Abraham His friend.

His was the peace that inspired Isaiah to poetry and comforted weeping Jeremiah.

His was the peace that permitted Him to sleep on the deck of a ship in a stormy sea.

His peace came from obedience to the Father's will. "His will is our peace."

His peace He gives to us.

BIBLE READING *II Corinthians 13*
MEMORY VERSE *John 16:33*

"Cast not away therefore your confidence, which hath great recompense of reward. For ye have need of patience, that, after ye have done the will of God, ye might receive the promise."

Hebrews 10:35, 36 (KJ)

ISN'T IT HARD to be patient?

We're so often impatient with others. They're not so perfect as we expect them to be and we're disappointed. We forget that God is patiently making them into what He wants them to be and that they're not finished yet. We expect others to show more perfection than we show.

We are impatient with ourselves. We fail, so we give up.

We forget that we will be perfect when we are with the Lord Jesus and are like Him forever. We forget that it takes time to make us what He wants us to be.

And we are impatient with God. He is answering our prayers, yet we don't give Him time to show us the answer. We quit praying and despair.

Yet our patient God is never impatient with us!

BIBLE READING   *Jude*
MEMORY VERSE   *Hebrews 10:35, 36*

"That which we have seen and heard we proclaim also to you, so that you may have fellowship with us; and our fellowship is with the Father and with his Son Jesus Christ."

I John 1:3

Do YOU KNOW the wonder of the peace of God in you?
Does the precious Name of Jesus thrill your soul just through and
    through?
Have you known the joy of serving Him in nursing tasks you do?
Then let's be friends together! Let me walk awhile with you!
By His great and sovereign power He makes blinded eyes to see;
We can share the freedom with which Christ has made the sinner
    free.
Some day, nursing over, in His Heavenly Home we'll be.
So let's read and pray together, Nurse . . . Come, walk awhile with
    me!

BIBLE READING   *Matthew 1*
MEMORY VERSE   *I John 1:3*

"O magnify the Lord with me, and let us exalt his name together. I sought the Lord, and he answered me, and delivered me from all my fears."

Psalm 34:3, 4

TOGETHER! What nurse hasn't learned the value of teamwork? Is there a patient too heavy to lift? Let's do it together. Is there a procedure of which I'm not sure? I find someone who knows, and we do it together. Is there a shortage of help and is everyone overburdened with work? The work gets lighter as we do it together.

So it is with praising and serving God. We who are "seated *together* in heavenly places in Christ" are to be together also in our service here.

Do you know another Christian nurse? Find a way to help her today. Share your blessings. Is there a Christian patient on your ward? Maybe she would like you to take time to pray with her today.

BIBLE READING   *Matthew 2*
MEMORY VERSE   *Psalm 34:3, 4*

MAY 3

"Thy people shall be willing in the day of thy power, in the beauties of holiness from the womb of the morning: thou hast the dew of thy youth."

Psalm 110:3 (KJ)

A LINE from a prayer offered at our graduation service has helped me ever since. "Help us to know Thy will," the pastor prayed, "and to do it with gladness."

A very talented nurse who works grudgingly can never give the nursing care a willing nurse can give, however inexperienced she may be.

The Lord Jesus wants our willing service, and He is able to show His power in us when we are willing to do His will. When He shows you His will for your life, are you willing to do it?

BIBLE READING   *Matthew 3*
MEMORY VERSE   *Psalm 110:3*

MAY 4

". . . that you may declare the wonderful deeds of him who called you out of darkness into his marvelous light."

I Peter 2:9b

MOST OF US are proud of the hospital we serve. All of us contribute to its reputation by the kind of nursing care we give.

"That's a good hospital," people say. "I know a really good nurse from there." Or they say, "I wouldn't go to that hospital. The nurses there are people I wouldn't want taking care of me!"

If you are a Christian nurse, you also represent the Church of Jesus Christ and people will judge its service by the kind of service you give.

Study I Peter 2:9-25. List some ways you represent the people of God as you depend on Him and obey these instructions.

BIBLE READING   *Matthew 4*
MEMORY VERSE   *I Peter 2:9*

MAY 5

"Ye also helping together by prayer for us, that for the gift bestowed upon us by the means of many persons thanks may be given by many on our behalf . . . Not for that we have dominion over your faith, but we are helpers of your joy: for by faith ye stand."

II Corinthians 1:11, 24

"HELPING by prayer . . . ," "helpers of your joy . . . ."

Many nurses every year write their reason for wanting to be a nurse: "because I want to help people." We help the doctor to effect a cure by helping the patient to follow his orders; we help the helpless and we help those who need to learn to help themselves.

As Christian nurses we can help people in an eternal way, for the power of God is made available to us as we pray for others. How wonderful that we can help people to find real joy, showing them the joy of the Lord Jesus as our motive for helping them.

BIBLE READING   *Matthew 5*
MEMORY VERSE   *II Corinthians 1:11*

MAY 6

"Gather the people together, men, and women, and children, and thy stranger that is within thy gates, that they may hear, and that they may learn, and fear the Lord your God, and observe to do all the words of this law: And that their children, which have not known anything, may hear, and learn to fear the Lord your God, as long as ye live in the land whither ye go over Jordan to possess it."

Deuteronomy 31:12, 13 (KJ)

FOUR REASONS for group Bible study are given in these verses. All the people were to get together to listen to God's Word, to learn His Word, to learn to reverence Him, and to learn to do what He commanded.

Ask the Lord what He would have you do about a Bible study among the nurses that you know. Are you attending a group Bible study? Are you bringing others, even strangers, to hear the Word of God? Do you listen reverently, and concentrate? Do you sometimes contribute to the study the things God seems to be teaching you? When there is a command to obey, are you careful to do it right away?

BIBLE READING   *Matthew 6*
MEMORY VERSE   *Deuteronomy 31:12, 13*

MAY 7

"Brethren, if a man is overtaken in any trespass, you who are spiritual should restore him in a spirit of gentleness. Look to yourself, lest you too be tempted." "If your brother sins against you, go and tell him his fault between you and him alone. If he listens to you, you have gained your brother."

Galatians 6:1, Matthew 18:15

WHEN I was a student nurse, my favorite instructor was one who always pointed out my mistakes yet also let me know that she believed I could and would improve.

In our Christian fellowship we often become aware of the faults and failures of others. It is easy to criticize. It takes real Christian grace to forgive. It is easy to see the faults of others; it is hard to sense our own weakness. It is easy to be discouraged when another Christian fails. It takes a really spiritual Christian to adopt a hopeful attitude toward that one and to restore him to fellowship.

Real Christian love never fails.

BIBLE READING   *Matthew 7*
MEMORY VERSE   *Galatians 6:1*

MAY 8

"And he said unto her, 'Daughter, your faith has made you well; go in peace.'"
Luke 8:48

THE LORD JESUS knows all about the work of nurses. He spent time with the sick and handicapped. He healed them.

Study these verses about His care for the sick and disabled:

Mark 6:54-56

Luke 5:17-25; 6:6-11; 8:43-48; 14:1-6; 18:35-43

Most wonderful of all, the Lord Jesus effected a cure for the malignant disease of sin. We are all sick with sin and none of us can cure himself. Sin is a disease which leaves it victim handicapped for life. Some are blind to spiritual realities; some are deaf to the voice of God; others are unable to walk and work for God because of this terrible affliction. When Jesus died on the cross He bore the sin of the whole world. All you need to do is to turn from your sin and trust Him to release you from its handicap. He will give you sight and hearing and the ability to walk with Him in ways of spiritual blessings. He will give you life . . . eternal life. Won't you let Him be your Savior from sin today?

BIBLE READING   *Matthew 8*
MEMORY VERSE   *Luke 8:48*

MAY 9

"Epaphras, who is one of yourselves, a servant of Christ Jesus, greets you, always remembering you earnestly in his prayers, that you may stand mature and fully assured in all the will of God."

Colossians 4:12

THE MEANING of this Christian's name is probably "lovely." Does the loveliness of the Lord Jesus shine from our lives as Christian nurses?

Epaphras' work was not the sort to make him famous or rich; probably most of it was done in secret. He prayed earnestly, laboring in prayer (another translation says "wrestling for you"). Notice the prayer he dared to pray for God's people.

Ask God to make the Christian nurses in your locality "stand mature and fully assured in all the will of God."

BIBLE READING   *Matthew 9*
MEMORY VERSE   *Colossians 4:12*

MAY 10

". . . Christ in you, the hope of glory."

Colossians 1:27

OF ALL the ways He shows Himself, the dearest
Is when Christ lives in those we're living nearest.
He comes again to us in human guise
Who knows the dimness of our earthbound eyes.
Sensing how doubts beset our finest choices,
He speaks to us in quiet earthly voices;
He sees how quick we are to go astray,
And uses friends to help us find the way.
Oh, He was lonely once. He understands
How dear the loving help of human hands.

—Wheaton Alumni News

BIBLE READING   *Matthew 10*
MEMORY VERSE   *Colossians 1:27*

". . . and in this place will I give peace, saith the Lord of hosts."

Haggai 2:9 (KJ)

"IN THIS place will I give peace . . ."
Where shall He give peace?
In the hurry, hardness and hushed heartache of a hectic hospital day?
In the drab dullness of drudgery?
In the restlessness of rooming with the wrong roommate?
In hours of wondering and wishing to know the future?
In weakness and inadequacy for the work one has to do?
In trials and temptations?
In a host of unsympathetic friends?
In little irritations and petty difficulties?
"In this place will I give peace, saith the Lord of hosts . . ."

"Now may the Lord of peace himself give you peace at all times in all ways" (II Thessalonians 3:16).

BIBLE READING   *Matthew 11*
REVIEW MEMORY VERSES

"Trust in the Lord with all your heart, and do not rely on your own insight. In all your ways acknowledge him, and he will make straight your paths."

Proverbs 3:5, 6

GOD'S GUIDANCE is very practical. He knows you better than you know yourself, better than your closest friend knows you. He knows what your real desires and needs are.

He guides your paths according to what *He* is like: understanding, loving, strong, and very wise. He wants the very best for you. He loves your family better than you do, and He is the only one who can really solve the problems of your friends. He cares enough about you to want you to choose the right course, the right profession, the right friends.

He guides you, too, according to what *you* are like. He knows what circumstances will mean something to you. He knows your past, and your whole future. He knows how you think, and what kind of writing you are interested in reading.

Do you know anyone else you could trust to direct you so wisely?

BIBLE READING   *Matthew 12*
MEMORY VERSE   *Proverbs 3:5,6*

MAY 13

"Then he said, 'Do not come near; put off your shoes from your feet, for the place on which you are standing is holy ground."

Exodus 3:5

RIGHT WHERE you are! Not only in church or in your fellowship group or in your quiet time . . . not only when you feel the presence of God with you . . . not only when you are reading His Word or talking with another Christian.

He is there right where you are on duty in that difficult spot, and so it is holy ground, ground to be claimed for His use, whose it is and whose you are.

Right where you are, worship Him. Right where you are, serve Him.

Right where you are is your mission field today.

BIBLE READING   *Matthew 13*
REVIEW MEMORY VERSES

MAY 14

"The Lord said to Moses, 'Why do you cry to me? Tell the people of Israel to go forward.'"

Exodus 14:15

SOMETIMES we shouldn't pray! When God has given a command to obey, you had better do what He has commanded. Disobedience cannot claim answers to prayer. A disobedient heart cannot really pray.

Ask God to search your heart today and show you anything there that may be hindering His answering your prayers. Take time to listen to His voice.

Perhaps as well as crying to Him to save people in your hospital He wants you to speak of Him to them. Maybe instead of asking Him for leading for tomorrow He wants you to follow His guidance for today!

BIBLE READING *Matthew 14*
REVIEW MEMORY VERSES

MAY 15

" 'O Lord God, thou hast only begun to show thy servant thy greatness and thy mighty hand; for what god is there in heaven or on earth who can do such works and mighty acts as thine?' "

Deuteronomy 3:24

ALL THAT YOU have learned about God and the Lord Jesus is just the beginning.

He has just *begun* to show you His greatness, for you have just begun to learn how small and weak you are. He has just begun to show you His power, for you have just begun to rely on His strength. He has just begun to show you that He is all you need for every minute of every day, for you have just begun to turn away from the idols of sin and self which have been controlling your minutes.

"He who has begun a good work in you will complete it."

"My Lord and my God!"

BIBLE READING *Matthew 15*
MEMORY VERSE *Deuteronomy 3:24*

MAY 16

"And I am sure that he who began a good work in you will bring it to completion at the day of Jesus Christ."

Philippians 1:6

IF YOU BEGIN a treatment you expect, unless something unforeseen comes up, to finish it. If you begin to care for a patient, you expect to finish the job.

In this verse we are told that the Lord Jesus who has begun "a good work" in us will go on completing it. He will not leave us alone until He has made us like Himself.

He may use circumstances and things which seem to us to be queer, frightening instruments for doing the job; but we are only laymen in understanding His professional equipment.

It is enough to know that He will finish what He has begun. Read Genesis 28:15.

BIBLE READING *Matthew 16*
MEMORY VERSE *Philippians 1:6*

MAY 17

"For if the readiness is there it is acceptable according to what a man has, not according to what he has not."

II Corinthians 8:12

SOMETIMES the Lord calls us to do something which seems to be far out of line with our talents and abilities. We shrink from doing it. "I can't lead that meeting!" "I can't witness!" "Me do that? Oh, no!"

Be careful that your "can't" isn't merely "won't" spelled differently. If you are ready and willing to give what you have, God will supply what you do not have.

Sometimes people hesitate to come to the Lord Jesus for salvation because they are afraid that they will not be able to be the kind of Christians they want to be. All He wants is our willingness to let Him come into our hearts. He will make us what He wants us to be if we are willing to let Him.

Are you willing to let Him live in your heart today?

BIBLE READING *Matthew 17*
MEMORY VERSE *II Corinthians 8:12*

"O Lord, let thy ear be attentive to the prayer of thy servant . . . ."

Nehemiah 1:11

READ Nehemiah 1:5-11. This is the prayer which Nehemiah prayed for God's people. You can use this kind of prayer as you pray for Christian nurses today:

First, he praised God.

Second, he prayed for God's people.

Third, he confessed his sins.

Fourth, he brought a promise and laid it before the Lord.

And finally, he put God's people in God's hand and left them there.

He was persistent in prayer, he was deeply concerned and he prayed believing. Think about these verses before you pray today.

BIBLE READING *Matthew 18*
REVIEW MEMORY VERSES

"While they were talking and discussing together, Jesus himself drew near and went with them."

Luke 24:15

> WE SPOKE of little common things that night,
> The weather, and the washing; if 'twas right
> To hope for sunshine in a week so wet,
> And all the things we'd done since last we met.
> Then someone mentioned overcoming power.
> We talked of Jesus Christ a quiet hour.
> About our house, at common tasks we walked.
> Jesus Himself drew near us as we talked.
> Jesus Himself, the Master! Can it be
> He loves to be a Guest of you and me?

BIBLE READING *Matthew 19*
MEMORY VERSE *Luke 24:15*

MAY 20

"Blessed be the Lord! for he has heard the voice of my supplications."
Psalm 28:6

GOD LETS US see the lives and problems of others so that we may help them. We may help by something we do or something we say or (and this is the most help of all) simply by quietly praying for them. Isn't it strange how easy it is to criticize, how hard it is to pray?

When we pray for others we claim the victory which the Lord Jesus won on Calvary by dying for them. When we pray, Satan is defeated.

Christian nurses know the problem of the medical profession well enough to be real prayer warriors in this field. Pray today for Christian doctors and nurses. Pray for wisdom for them in their work. Pray that they may be used of God in their profession to win others to Him.

Ask God to make you a real witness for Him in your nursing today.

BIBLE READING   *Matthew 20*
MEMORY VERSE   *Psalm 28:6*

MAY 21

"Know therefore this day, and consider it in thine heart, that the Lord he is God in heaven above, and upon the earth beneath: there is none else."
Deuteronomy 4:39 (KJ)

KNOW IT, today. Know it in your mind and know it in your heart. Consider the implications of your faith that "the Lord, He is God."

You'll find a cure for anxiety if you stop to think about who He is who cares for you.

It is a cure for worry about the future, for He is the eternal God. It is a cure for worry about the past, for He is the God who has forgiven your sins and brought you into His family. And it is a cure for worry about the present, for if the past and the future belong to Him, surely you can trust Him to be doing something wonderful for you and in you today, too.

BIBLE READING   *Matthew 21*
MEMORY VERSE   *Deuteronomy 4:39*

100

"And from his fulness have we all received, grace upon grace."

John 1:16

GRACE UPON grace . . . more and more grace . . . all that we need.

Many years ago a friend gave me a short poem about God's giving grace for each added burden. Recently I had it on my desk and she happened to see it.

"That's just what I need today," she said. "Where did you get it?"

Grace for grace — and that sufficient.

BIBLE READING   *Matthew 22*
MEMORY VERSE   *John 1:16*

"Beloved, if our hearts do not condemn us, we have confidence before God; and whatsoever we ask, we receive of him, because we keep his commandments, and do those things that are pleasing in his sight."

I John 3:21, 22

GOD'S CARDIOLOGY department classifies our hearts as "deceitful above all things" and "desperately wicked." How then can we have hearts that "condemn us not"?

John 3:18 gives the answer: "He who believes on Him [God's Son] is not condemned."

And "There is therefore now no condemnation for those who are in Christ Jesus."

Have you put your trust in God's Son, the Lord Jesus? Are you believing on Him? Then you are "in Christ." And there is no condemnation for you.

His blood cleanses us from all sin. With clean hearts we turn to God with confidence and know that He will answer our prayer.

Pray today for that personal need which only God and you know about.

BIBLE READING   *Matthew 23*
MEMORY VERSE   *I John 3:21, 22*

MAY 24

"'What man is there that is fearful and fainthearted? Let him go back to his house, lest the heart of his fellows melt as his heart.'"

Deuteronomy 20:8

IT IS A GOOD IDEA to keep discouragement between ourselves and the Lord. If you are afraid, tell Him about your fear and ask Him to take away your faintheartedness.

Telling others about our fears may make them fearful too; telling them about our discouragement may only discourage them.

Do not undertake any work for God until you have asked Him for the courage necessary. Let Him say to you, "Fear not! I am thy shield and thy exceeding great reward."

BIBLE READING   *Matthew 24*
REVIEW MEMORY VERSES

MAY 25

". . . and serve Him only . . . ."

I Samuel 7:3

THIS VERSE could well hang on the wall of every Christian nurse's room.

"Serve Him only." The demands upon us as nurses are always multiple. We must please patients and doctors and keep our fellow nurses happy. We must remember the other departments . . . so that we do not make more work for the diet kitchen, the laundry, the laboratory, or X-ray. Sometimes we wail that we just can't please everybody!

No, we can't. But if we are serving Him only, our God will see that our work is done with a minimum of fuss and a maximum of efficiency. And serving Him is the best service that we can give to others.

BIBLE READING   *Matthew 25*
REVIEW MEMORY VERSES

"I am the Lord who sanctify you."

Leviticus 20:8

THE BIBLE CALLS us a special people (I Peter 2:9, Deuteronomy 7:6), chosen to belong to God, His own possession. We will be different from those who do not know our God; we will be "set apart" for Him.

Isn't it hard to be different? It's so much easier to go with the group and follow the prevailing standards of right and wrong — white and black and gray — than to follow the moral law of the Bible. Sometimes as Christians we wish to be as much like others as possible. Or we withdraw into a little Christian clique, where we are "set apart," certainly, but set apart for our own selfish friendships and fellowship, not set apart for God and His purpose for a lost world.

Are you living as one who is "set apart" for God today? Remember . . . "The Lord your God has chosen you to be a people for his own possession."

BIBLE READING *Matthew 26*
REVIEW MEMORY VERSES

"I will cry unto God most high; unto God that performeth all things for me."
Psalm 57:2 (KJ)

IN SOME TRANSLATIONS, the word "performeth" in this verse reads "perfecteth." If God is doing it, it must be perfect. Another translation reads, "I cry to God . . . who fulfils his purpose for me."

The God who lives in your heart is the One who will perform and perfect all things for you today. You may meet things which are too hard for you. Maybe some things which seem easy will turn out to be difficult. Perhaps you will meet things which will try your patience or worry you; then you will want to read Psalm 57:1 and rest peacefully in the shadow of the everlasting wings, knowing that He will perfect all things for you, and fulfil His purpose.

Make it your habit to pray about everything you meet.

BIBLE READING   *Matthew 27*
MEMORY VERSE   *Psalm 57:2*

MAY 28

"To you therefore who believe, he is precious . . . ."

I Peter 2:7

MORE precious is He than He was when I met Him
That day when He lifted me, wounded, half dead,
As I lay by the road that led down to destruction —
He took me to shelter and blessing instead.

More precious is He than He was when He led me
Across the green pastures through sunshiny days,
When all life was joy and happy thanksgiving
He "robed me with gladness" and "girded with praise."

Precious, more precious, most precious, this Savior,
Whatever I treasure, I value Him more.
I dwell in His safety, for He watches o'er me —
He's daily more precious than ever before.

BIBLE READING   *Matthew 28*
MEMORY VERSE   *I Peter 2:7*

MAY 29

"Does he not see my ways, and number all my steps?"

Job 31:4

WHEN YOU ARE looking to God for guidance, there are some
practical steps you can take.

Pray. Ask God to give you a willingness to do whatever it is
He shows you to be His will.

Read. God will not direct you to do something which He has forbidden you to do in His Word. Think over what you read, and be sure that you understand His commands and can apply them in practical ways to what you are doing or saying.

Study biography, books about careers you might be interested in, missionary literature, the news. Helpful books on almost any subject are readily available to most of us.

Write. Inquire about possible openings for you. Get all the information you can.

Think. Use the mind God has given you and assess what resources you have that He might use in His world.

Ask. Talk with people who may know more than you do about the opportunities in certain fields of service.

Above all, *trust*. Trust God as you seek to find out all you can. Trust Him as you pray. Trust Him as you think and try to assess your own talents. (He may surprise you by showing you some you didn't know you had!) Be ambitious for God. Ask Him to make you someone better than you could ever be alone. Take steps to do all God wants you to do with the one life He has given you.

BIBLE READING *Psalms 142, 143*
MEMORY VERSE *Job 31:4*

MAY 30

"And when Samuel had heard all the words of the people, he repeated them in the ears of the Lord." "So Samuel told all the words of the Lord to the people . . . ."

I Samuel 8:21, 10

HERE'S AN EXAMPLE for us to follow today. When we hear the complaints and questions and doubts of others it's easy to join in with our own until the doubts and unhappinesses spread to the whole group. When the Lord speaks to us, it is all too easy to forget to tell others what He has said.

When Samuel heard the words of the people, he told the Lord. When he heard the words of the Lord, he told the people.

Be God's messenger to those with whom you work today. And

be His prayer warrior, too, bringing Him the needs of those around you as you sense and observe them.

BIBLE READING   *Psalms 144, 145, 146*
REVIEW MEMORY VERSES

MAY 31

"Saul also went to his home at Gibeah, and with him went men of valor whose hearts God had touched.   But some worthless fellows said, 'How can this man save us?'   And they despised him, and brought him no present. But he held his peace."

I Samuel 10:26, 27

SAUL in these verses is a picture of the Lord Jesus. Gibeah means "hill," and it reminds us of the hill, Calvary.

There the world, the worthless fellows, despised Him. But He held his peace. Compare these verses with Matthew 26:23 and Mark 14:61.

What presents did the men whose hearts God had touched bring to Saul? I wonder if the gift of their hearts, their love and loyalty, wasn't the greatest present they could bring?

Our Lord Jesus values our hearts more than any other gift. God doesn't want our presents; He wants us!

BIBLE READING   *Psalms 147, 148, 149*
REVIEW MEMORY VERSES

"But according to his promise we wait for new heavens and a new earth in which righteousness dwells. Therefore, beloved, since you wait for these, be zealous to be found by him in peace, without spot, or blemish, and at peace."

II Peter 3:13, 14

WE NURSES won't be necessary, over there in Heaven.
The people there are healthy and there isn't any death.
The pains that we are easing now will all be gone, in Glory,
And nurses can take off their shoes and stop to catch their breath.

There won't be any nursing care that we can give in Heaven.
We won't be giving intravenous fluids there, or pills,
Inhabitants of Heaven, we shall run and not be weary,
But they won't be needing nurses, for there won't be any ills.

We nurses won't be necessary, over there in Heaven.
If we want to serve God as a nurse, this earth's the only place.
The only time we're needed is today, while folks are suffering,
For they won't need any nurses when they see the Savior's face.

BIBLE READING *Psalm 1, Revelation 11*
MEMORY VERSE *II Peter 3:13, 14*

"For in Christ Jesus neither circumcision availeth anything, nor uncircumcision, but a new creature."

Galatians 6:15 (KJ)

"IN CHRIST JESUS . . . a new creature!"

Let the Lord Jesus Christ make you His own today. Bring Him your sin for His forgiveness. Bring Him your helplessness and your great need of Him. He will give you new life in Him, new faith in Him, new attitudes, new aims. You will find that you are learning to rely on Another, the Lord Jesus Christ.

Every nurse relies on orders. The more difficult and complex her task, the more she needs the help of the physician.

The strength of the Christian is in reliance on Another. We are all very new nurses in God's sick world, and it is only as He is able to work through us that we can be of use to Him.

The book of Galatians says a great deal about reliance upon Christ as the One who is all we need. You will find

Christ, our deliverance: 1:3, 4
Christ, our life: 2:20
Christ in us, we in Him: 3:26, 27
Christ, our freedom: 5:1

BIBLE READING   *Psalm 2, Revelation 12*
MEMORY VERSE   *Galatians 6:15*

JUNE 3

"And every one who was in distress, and every one who was in debt, and every one who was discontented, gathered to him, and he became captain over them. And there were with him about four hundred men. . . . 'Stay with me, fear not; for he that seeks my life seeks your life; with me you shall be in safekeeping.'"

I Samuel 22:2, 23

DAVID'S FOUR HUNDRED brought their burdens of discontent, distress, and debt to him. They were with him, and he told them, "Fear not; for . . . with me you shall be in safekeeping."

The Captain of our salvation, the Lord Jesus, calls us to Himself with our burdens.

Are you discontented today? Are you distressed with the load of work and worry that is on your shoulders? Is the burden of your sin too great to bear?

Come to the Lord Jesus with it all. Tell Him you need Him to take away your sin and make you His own; tell Him that you will let Him take charge and be "Captain" of your life.

The unrest of all the world cannot touch you if you are abiding in Him. He is the only safety for now and for eternity.

BIBLE READING   *Psalm 3, Revelation 13*
REVIEW MEMORY VERSES

JUNE 4

"Then the people rejoiced because these had given willingly, for with a whole heart they offered freely to the Lord; David the king also rejoiced greatly."
I Chronicles 29:9

AN UNWILLING heart doubles the drudgery of any task. An unwilling helper makes the work harder. How many times we say, "I'd rather do it myself . . . it would be easier than with that kind of assistance."

A willing nurse, even if she is just a beginning student, can be a real joy to work with.

I wonder if it is possible to serve God half-heartedly, or if half-heartedness may be a sign that we are serving ourselves or others instead of Him? Only the willing-hearted have joy in Christian service.

Our King, like David, rejoices when His people willingly offer themselves and all they have, with whole and perfect hearts, to Him.

BIBLE READING   *Psalm 4, Revelation 14*
REVIEW MEMORY VERSES

JUNE 5

" 'I am the Alpha and the Omega, the beginning and the end. To the thirsty I will give water without price from the fountain of the water of life.' "
Revelation 21:6

WHATEVER YOUR THIRST, the water of life which the Lord Jesus gives can quench it.

Perhaps you are looking for security. Read Psalm 37:1-3. Maybe you need rest. Read Matthew 11:28, 29. Sometimes the heart is thirsty for peace. Then it's good to look at John 16:33.

Or you may be longing for a Friend to help you do what you yourself cannot do. Study John 15:15, 16.

God promises to supply your every need when you come to Him through His Son.

Read the verse at the top of the page again. Trust Him to do as He has promised.

BIBLE READING   *Psalm 5, Revelation 15*
MEMORY VERSE   *Revelation 21:6*

JUNE 6

"He who made the Pleiades and Orion, and turns deep darkness into the morning, and darkens the day into night: who calls for the waters of the sea, and pours them out upon the surface of the earth, the Lord is his name."

Amos 5:8

> God's stars come out when the sun has set . . .
> Night duty may be your best time yet!
> On dark night duty you can show
> God's lamp, God's love, for of course you know
> When you are "on nights" it's time to light
> Your way with truth and faith and right.
> Night duty gives a chance to keep
> A quiet heart for a good day's sleep.
> Night duty is a time when you
> Can prove God's faithfulness anew.
> Tired and weary, you long for rest,
> Yet stop and pray, and do your best
> And rest in Him.   Then you'll never doubt
> When the sun goes down, God's stars come out!

BIBLE READING   *Psalm 6, Revelation 16*
MEMORY VERSE   *Amos 5:8*

" 'Oh that they had such a mind as this always, to fear me and to keep all my commandments, that it might go well with them, and with their children forever!' "

Deuteronomy 5:29

GOD IS a careful Physician who gives orders intended for the welfare of His patients and their families. If you ask Him why He has done certain things, this may be all the answer you will get.

People sometimes fear to obey the Lord because they expect Him to give them a difficult and joyless life. They are afraid that His orders will not always be for their good.

Yet God so wanted the welfare of His world that He gave His Son to die in order to change our condition from "moribund" to "more abundantly alive!"

Turn your case over to Him today, and let Him give your orders.

BIBLE READING   *Psalm 7, Revelation 17*
MEMORY VERSE   *Deuteronomy 5:29*

"Go and proclaim these words toward the north, and say, 'Return, faithless Israel, says the Lord. I will not look on you in anger, for I am merciful, says the Lord; I will not be angry for ever. Only acknowledge your guilt, that you rebelled against the Lord your God, and scattered your favors among strangers under every green tree, and that you have not obeyed my voice, says the Lord.' " "Your iniquities have turned these away, and your sins have kept good things from you . . ."

Jeremiah 3:12, 13; 5:25

SOME NURSES start out well on their nursing career. Each treatment is done carefully and gladly. Patients are left comfortable, and even overtime is accepted with cheerfulness.

Later on they lose interest in their work and it becomes half-done drudgery. Nobody enjoys the service of a half-hearted nurse . . . least of all the nurse herself!

All the excuses or reasons for this unhappy state do not improve it. Wishing things were different doesn't help. Only a determined effort can restore the nurse's happiness in her work.

Backsliding, faithless Christians are in a pitiful state of half-heartedness, too. Their sins keep them from enjoying God, and their stubbornness keeps them from obeying Him. These verses give the remedy for this condition. What is it?

BIBLE READING *Psalm 8, Revelation 18*
REVIEW MEMORY VERSES

JUNE 9

"And Samuel said, 'Has the Lord as great delight in burnt offerings and sacrifices, as in obeying the voice of the Lord? Behold, to obey is better than sacrifice, and to hearken than the fat of rams.'"

I Samuel 15:22

BECAUSE OUR WORK is hard and the need of patients so great, it is sometimes easy for us to fall into the habit of self-sacrifice to the point of disobedience. Then we become self-appointed martyrs, unhappy because overworked, yet somehow unable to share the burden with others. We give our whole lives to nursing rather than to God.

There is such a thing as giving too much of ourselves to His service and too little of ourselves to Him.

No matter how heavy the load, we should be conscious of our need to hear His voice and obey Him. No matter how full the days, there must be time to spend with God. If the burden seems heavy and the yoke hard, then it must be a self-chosen burden, not of Him; for Jesus said, "My yoke is easy and my burden is light."

BIBLE READING *Psalm 9, Revelation 19*
MEMORY VERSE *I Samuel 15:22*

"Seek the Lord while he may be found, call upon him while he is near; let the wicked forsake his way, and the unrighteous man his thoughts; let him return to the Lord, that he may have mercy on him, and to our God, for he will abundantly pardon. For my thoughts are not your thoughts, neither are your ways my ways, saith the Lord."

Isaiah 55:6-8

COME to the Savior now, He gently calleth thee;
In true repentance bow, before Him bend thy knee;
He waiteth to bestow salvation, peace and love,
True joy on earth below, a home in heaven above.
Come to the Savior now, ye who have wandered far;
Renew your solemn vow, for His by right you are;
Come like poor wandering sheep returning to His fold;
His arm will safely keep, His love will ne'er grow cold.
Come to the Savior now! He offers all to thee,
And in His merits thou hast an unfailing plea.
No vain excuses frame, for feelings do not stay;
None who to Jesus came were ever sent away.
Come to the Savior, all, whate'er your burdens be;
Hear now His loving call, "Cast all your care on Me."
Come, and for every grief in Jesus you will find
A sure and safe relief, a loving friend and kind.

John M. Wigner

BIBLE READING   *Psalm 10, Revelation 20*
MEMORY VERSE   *Isaiah 55:6-8*

"My sons, do not now be negligent, for the Lord has chosen you to stand in his presence, to minister to him, and to be his ministers and burn incense to him."

2 Chronicles 29:11

NEGLECT can be held responsible for many deaths. The little infection that became staphylococcic . . . the common cold that turned into pneumonia . . . the tiny lump that became a fatal carcinoma. Nurses know the danger of neglect.

We who belong to the Lord Jesus are cautioned against being neglectful in spiritual things. Like the Levites, we are chosen to stand before the Lord. We must not neglect our service, we must not neglect our ministry to others, and we must not neglect to worship Him.

And we must not neglect the little sins that would estrange us from Him, either. Turn today from the little prayerlessness, the little lack of study, the little disobediences.

"Do not now be negligent . . . for the Lord has chosen you"!

BIBLE READING *Psalm 11, Revelation 21*
REVIEW MEMORY VERSES

JUNE 12

"He is the head of the body, the church; he is the beginning, the firstborn from the dead, that in everything he might be pre-eminent."
Colossians 1:18

SOME OF US want to be both patient and physician, diagnosing and prescribing for the spiritual ills that beset our souls. Sometimes we call in the Lord Jesus as consultant, but if we do not like His medicines or His treatments we go back to caring for ourselves, ignoring His orders. And we are not cured.

For a Christian there is only one Physician, the Lord Jesus, and He is given full charge of the case. He will show you the prophylaxis for many spiritual diseases. If you should contract discouragement, defeat, failure, sin, unhappiness or any other malady of the soul, He will restore you to health again.

Will you let Him have complete charge of your case today?

BIBLE READING *Psalm 12, Revelation 22*
MEMORY VERSE *Colossians 1:18*

"Not that I have already obtained this or am already perfect; but I press on to make it my own, because Christ Jesus has made me his own."

Philippians 3:12

IN NURSING, there are many skills which we may learn about from our study, but until we have done them with our hands and practiced them we cannot say that we know them.

In the Christian life, there is always some new skill to learn, always something new to make our own in daily living.

Read Ephesians 6 and list the things which you can make your own in practical Christian living today.

BIBLE READING *Psalm 13*
MEMORY VERSE *Philippians 3:12*

"Commit your work to the Lord, and your plans shall be established."

Proverbs 16:3

TAKE TIME today to commit nursing as a whole to the Lord. Commit your work to Him, and those for whom you are caring. Commit the work of the other nurses in your hospital to Him.

Many nurses have positions of great responsibility; many are in dangerous places. Some are ill and fretting over work they cannot do. Pray for them today and commit their work to Him.

Another translation of "commit" is "roll." Roll the entire weight of your work on Him today. He will quiet your thoughts and accomplish much more than you could ever hope or plan.

BIBLE READING *Psalm 14*
MEMORY VERSE *Proverbs 16:3*

JUNE 15

" 'But seek first his kingdom and his righteousness, and all these things shall be yours as well.' "

Matthew 6:33

GIVE GOD the best of your day, and He will arrange the rest of the time to the very best advantage!

> I sought to send the multitude away,
> Saying, "These multitudes, these things to do,
> Press in upon me when I try to pray,
> And crowd my busy day with duties too."
> God took an hour from me. It seemed too small,
> And yet that hour He blessed and brake until
> There were bright moments for each task, and all
> The fragments left for Him at evening still.
> If I had sent the crowding tasks away,
> I would have missed a miracle that day.

BIBLE READING *Psalm 15*
MEMORY VERSE *Matthew 6:33*

JUNE 16

"The blessing of the Lord makes rich, and he adds no sorrow with it."

Proverbs 10:22

HAPPINESS which depends on circumstances is apt to be very brief; circumstances are always changing. Happiness which depends on ourselves is similarly short-lived, for we are seldom the same from one hour to the next. Life itself is uncertain; there is a hint of sorrow in every joy.

There is wealth that is not of this world, though, and a happiness apart from ourselves. When the Lord blesses, "He adds no sorrow with it."

Seek His blessing on your life today.

BIBLE READING *Psalm 16*
REVIEW MEMORY VERSES

"So then there remains a sabbath rest for the people of God."

Hebrews 4:9

READ THE 58th chapter of Isaiah. What are the conditions given in this chapter for answered prayer? For light? For health? For guidance?

As you read verses 13 and 14, remember that the Sabbath is a picture of the rest into which every Christian may enter.

How can we honor the Lord?

This chapter gives a very solemn warning against those who talk as though they loved God, yet live as though they had never heard of Him.

Ask God to speak to you through His Word today.

BIBLE READING   *Psalm 17*
MEMORY VERSE   *Hebrews 4:9*

"You shall have a song as in the night when a holy feast is kept; and gladness of heart, as when one sets out to the sound of the flute to go to the mountain of the Lord, to the Rock of Israel."

Isaiah 30:29

YOU CAN HAVE a song in your heart on night duty. You can have gladness of heart for every nursing day. You can be strong when you alone are weak, for you can know the Mighty One.

Gladness of heart comes when we spend time with God in real prayer. We listen to His Word and let Him speak to us and show us all that is not right; we let Him give us power to put away from us the sins that mar our joy; we admit our absolute powerlessness and turn to Him to be to us all that we need, all that we cannot be.

Then we begin to know what it is to sing in the dark and be glad, really glad, deep in our hearts.

BIBLE READING   *Psalm 18*
MEMORY VERSE   *Isaiah 30:29*

JUNE 19

"I will arise and go to my father, and will say to him, 'Father, I have sinned against heaven and before you.'"

Luke 15:18

HAVE YOU EVER PERSISTED in your own way about a matter because it was so desperately important to you? Headstrong and self-willed, you ignored the warning lights of conscience, your Bible and wise friends, until suddenly you found yourself in a situation from which to retreat would involve costly humbling of your pride.

The only way back to fellowship with God and with other people is that taken by the Prodigal Son our Lord told about in Luke 15. He faced the hard facts of his foolishness and sin, went back to where he had left the right way, acknowledged his sin and asked forgiveness of his father whom he had wronged.

That desirable position after graduation . . . your growing friendship with that young man . . . how you will spend your summer vacation . . . tangled inter-personal relationships in your dorm: is there any situation in your own life at this moment which should cause you to return to the place at which you left the will of God behind?

"If we confess our sins, he is faithful and just, and will forgive our sins and cleanse us from all unrighteousness" (I John 1:9).

BIBLE READING *Psalm 19*
MEMORY VERSE *Luke 15:18*

JUNE 20

"Yea, thou art my lamp, O Lord, and my God lightens my darkness."

II Samuel 22:29

ALL CHRISTIANS are on call for night duty for the Lord Jesus. The world is dark, but we have been delivered from the power of darkness. Although we live in a world of night we are to "walk as children of the day."

The Lord is our Lamp and our Light; He gives us His Word, a night order book to follow.

God's night nurses must be in constant contact with the Great Physician, helping those in darkness to put their confidence in Him. (You can safely call Him at any hour too, for He never sleeps!)

Remember that in the morning we shall give our night report to Him. Will He say "well done" when He looks at our night duty for Him?

Read the special orders in the Psalm you are studying today.

BIBLE READING *Psalm 20*
REVIEW MEMORY VERSES

JUNE 21

" 'For the Son of man also came not to be served but to serve, and to give his life as a ransom for many.' "

Mark 10:45

YOU HAVE DEDICATED your life "not to be served, but to serve." As a nurse you will minister to many and your days will be given for others.

But only One could give His life a ransom for us, for only the Lord Jesus lived a perfect life and only He is both God and man.

Think of Him. Lord of lords, King of kings, yet He washed His disciples' feet. He fed the hungry and healed the sick. He touched the lepers and let His disciple lean on His bosom. Although weary with His journey, He helped the Samaritan woman who had lived an adulterous life.

He can understand the problem you will meet today. He loves and understands you and your patients. He wants to help you serve others today.

BIBLE READING *Psalm 21*
MEMORY VERSE *Mark 10:45*

JUNE 22

"The fear of man lays a snare, but he who trusts in the Lord is safe."

Proverbs 29:25

HAVE YOU ever been caught in this trap: if you do this, someone won't like it; if you don't do it, someone else will be offended. What will she think? What will he say? The criticism of others and the fear of it are Satan's snares all along our way.

However there is a way to avoid this trap. We can confess our fear of others and put our trust in the safety of the Lord.

You see, He wants to guide you out of the snares of the world around you. As you trust Him, He will remove your "fear of man."

BIBLE READING   *Psalm 22*
MEMORY VERSE   *Proverbs 29:25*

JUNE 23

". . . and whoever would be first among you must be slave."

Mark 10:44

LET'S WORK in the clinic for the visually handicapped today and study the case of the blind man in Mark 10:46-52. Read the case study carefully.

What indications can you find of the Lord's interest in the individual? Did the blind man recognize and face his own need? What was the influence of the crowd upon him? What was his response to the call of the Lord? (What do you answer when the Lord calls you?) What was the effect of faith on the man's condition?

When the blind man could see, what did he choose to do? Read prayerfully Ephesians 1:17-20.

BIBLE READING   *Psalm 23*
MEMORY VERSE   *Mark 10:44*

"And Samuel said to the people, 'Fear not; you have done all this evil, yet do not turn aside from following the Lord, but serve the Lord with all your heart; and do not turn aside after vain things, which cannot profit or save, for they are vain. For the Lord will not cast away his people for his great name's sake, because it has pleased the Lord to make you a people for himself. Moreover as for me, far be it from me that I should sin against the Lord by ceasing to pray for you; and I will instruct you in the good and the right way. Only fear the Lord, and serve him faithfully with all your heart; for consider what great things he has done for you.'"

I Samuel 12:20-24

DISCOURAGEMENT and defeat! How much easier it is to look into our hearts and think about our failures than to look to our Savior and His faithfulness.

If you have failed, don't hurt His love any more by turning away from Him in discouragement. He loves you still! Turn to Him with reverent trust, knowing that He is waiting to cleanse you; think about what He has done for you.

If others have failed, and God has allowed you to see their need, then follow the example of prayer that is given in these verses. Don't stop praying for them!

BIBLE READING   *Psalm 24*
REVIEW MEMORY VERSES

"A man's mind plans his way, but the Lord directs his steps."

Proverbs 16:9

EACH STEP of your way today is planned for you by the Lord. He has thrilling things to teach you about His love and faithfulness. He has serious things to say to you about yourself and others. Be quietly aware of His presence and His direction whatever you may be doing today.

Christian nurses have been directed by God into many places of service in the world. Pray that their hearts may be gladly obedient as they serve Him.

Pray for nurses in industrial nursing and in public health. Pray for private duty nurses in homes and hospitals. Pray for student nurses. Pray for nurses on each shift at your hospital.

Pray that you may be aware of the Lord's direction in whatever you are to do today.

BIBLE READING   *Psalm 25*
MEMORY VERSE   *Proverbs 16:9*

JUNE 26

"Have you not known? Have you not heard? The Lord is the everlasting God, the Creator of the ends of the earth. He does not faint or grow weary. His understanding is unsearchable. He gives power to the faint, and to him who has no might he increases strength. Even youths shall faint and be weary, and young men shall utterly fall exhausted; but they who wait for the Lord shall renew their strength, they shall mount up with wings like eagles, they shall run and not be weary, they shall walk and not faint."

Isaiah 40:28-31

SYNCOPE is due to a temporary loss of blood to the brain. That is why you help a patient to lower his head when he feels that he is going to faint.

Spiritually, too, the faint need to bow their heads. As we wait upon the Lord for strength, the blood of the Lord Jesus is applied to our souls' need; we are renewed in power by a few moments of quiet prayer.

Notice that it is to them that have no might that strength is increased, and that He giveth power to the faint. "They go from strength to strength."

BIBLE READING   *Psalm 26*
MEMORY VERSE   *Isaiah 40:30, 31*

" 'Not by might, nor by power, but by my Spirit, says the Lord of hosts . . . .
For whoever has despised the day of small things shall rejoice . . . .' "
Zechariah 4:6,10

SMALL things! A little break in technique, a little carelessness, a little fear instilled in a patient by a word from a nurse . . . small things.

A little word of comfort, a little touch of kindness, a little task well done . . . small things.

Yet nursing is made up of countless small things which add up to "total patient care."

The manna was a small thing, yet it still speaks to us of Christ. The sweet incense was beaten small for the altar, yet as we read of it we learn more of the fragrance of His character. The fishes that fed the multitude were small ones!

Even the small things that go to make up your day today can be used by God if you will let Him control your moments. And you, do you feel small and powerless? Let His Spirit have control of your whole self today.

BIBLE READING *Psalm 27*
REVIEW MEMORY VERSES

"And let the beauty of the Lord our God be upon us: and establish thou the work of our hands upon us; yea, the work of our hands, establish thou it."
Psalm 90:17 (KJ)

GOD, touch my hands with tenderness,
For many folk today
Have never known your gentleness
And kindness; so I pray,
Oh, teach my fingers carefulness;
Make their touch warm and true,
And as I'm waiting on the sick,
Lord, keep me serving You.

—Reprinted by permission of
RN: A JOURNAL FOR NURSES

JUNE 29

"Your iniquities have turned these away, and your sins have kept good from you." "No good thing does the Lord withhold from those who walk uprightly."
Jeremiah 5:25; Psalm 84:11

YOUR PATIENTS do not always know what is good for them. They sometimes believe that exercise is necessary when strict bed rest is the order; or they may believe that a different diet would be better than the one ordered for their condition. Usually those who are willing to rely on the doctor's judgment benefit.

Even more surely, those who obey the orders of the Great Physician and walk "uprightly" find that He withholds no good thing from them. It is our disobedience which withholds good things from us.

BIBLE READING   *Psalm 29*
REVIEW MEMORY VERSES

JUNE 30

". . . of beaten work shall the candlestick be made . . . ." "thou shalt make it a perfume, . . . and thou shalt beat some of it very small, and put of it before the testimony in the tabernacle of the congregation, where I will meet with thee . . . ." "And they did beat the gold into thin plates, and cut it into wires, to work it in the blue, and in the purple, and in the scarlet, and in the fine linen, with cunning work." "And if thou offer . . . of thy firstfruits unto the Lord, thou shalt offer . . . corn beaten out of full ears."
Exodus 25:31; 30:35,36; 39:3; Leviticus 2:14 (KJ)

BLOW BY BLOW the candlestick was made, beaten for beauty, beaten into a holder for light. Spices were beaten into perfume, fragrant for the service of God. Beaten gold went into the clothing of Aaron, the high priest. Beaten corn was part of the offering "made by fire" unto the Lord.

Beating, you see, may be the price we have to pay for giving light and fragrance and beauty and food to the people of God.

124

Unless we are willing to allow ourselves to become nothing, beaten small by the circumstances He sends to form us for His use, we shall be useless.

BIBLE READING *Psalm 30*
REVIEW MEMORY VERSES

JULY 1

"Now faith is the assurance of things hoped for, the conviction of things not seen."

Hebrews 11:1

THE NIGHT of our world was black.
No evening star . . .
No calling candlelight
From door ajar . . .
And yet we knew
(Bewildered round about)
Faith was a lantern to lead us on.
We dared not doubt.

Our hearts were dark with sin.
We had wandered far
From the hills of heavenly light
Where the Blessed are . . .
Yet now we know
(Though our lantern of faith is dim)
Jesus who lives is our Light of Life.
We dare trust Him.

BIBLE READING   *Psalm 31*
MEMORY VERSE   *Hebrews 11:1*

" 'The Lord your God who goes before you will himself fight for you, just as he did for you in Egypt before your eyes, and in the wilderness, where you have seen how the Lord your God bore you, as a man bears his son, in all the way that you went, until you came to this place.' "

Deuteronomy 1:30, 31

HERE is a name of our God which can be a real comfort when you are dreading some new assignment or some unknown way: "The Lord your God who goes before you!"

You can believe in Him for your future, not dreading or being afraid, because you know what He has been to you in the past. Such a comforting comparison . . . He carried you as a father carries his little boy . . . in his arms or high on his shoulders. Can't you just see the little boy laughing as he is carried by his father?

You can trust God to go before you in any new thing you face. He will go before you.

BIBLE READING   *Psalm 32*
MEMORY VERSE   *Deuteronomy 1:30, 31*

"And now, behold, we are in your hand: do as it seems good and right in your sight to do to us."

Joshua 9:25

As THE GIBEONITES were in the hand of Joshua, we too are in the hand of God. His love has conquered us and we belong to Him.

There are few organs as intricate and wonderful as the human hand. It is used for protection and for service. It is powerful yet can give the gentlest of caressing touches. It can be used on fine sewing or on large building projects. It can hold little things carefully and big things securely.

Think, then, of the hand of God. However small and insignificant you may feel, you are in His hand. However large and important the matter which concerns you, since that also is in His hand, it can be resolved.

Let this verse be your prayer of consecration today: "Do as it seems good and right in your sight to do to us."

BIBLE READING   *Psalm 33*
MEMORY VERSE   *Joshua 9:25*

JULY 4

"And a man shall be as an hiding place from the wind, and a covert from the tempest; as rivers of water in a dry place, as the shadow of a great rock in a weary land." "But there the glorious Lord will be unto us a place of broad rivers and streams; wherein shall go no galley with oars, neither shall gallant ship pass thereby. For the Lord is our judge, the Lord is our lawgiver, the Lord is our king; he will save us."

Isaiah 32:2; 33:21, 22 (KJ)

THESE are verses for a torrid summer day when scarcely a breeze is stirring and the work you do is harder because of the humid heat.

When the hot winds come and the summer storms, when there is no shade from the burning heat of the day, then there is a refuge for us that is better than any man-made air-conditioner . . . an eternal refuge, a calm, cool place of retreat for the troubled soul.

BIBLE READING   *Psalm 34*
MEMORY VERSE   *Isaiah 32:2*

JULY 5

" 'Fear not, O land; be glad and rejoice, for the Lord has done great things.' "
Joel 2:21

WE ARE WEAK and don't know what to do. We go to others for advice and are disappointed. We find that no one else can do for us what we cannot do for ourselves. And so we are afraid.

Then some wonderful day we look up and find that God has been waiting all the time for us to fix our eyes on Him. You see, He knows what to do and He is strong enough to do great things for us.

Pray today for Christian nurses on vacation, on days off, or off duty for other reasons. Pray that their eyes may be upon God today and that, wherever they may be, they will not forget that they belong to Him.

BIBLE READING   *Psalm 35*
REVIEW MEMORY VERSES

JULY 6

" 'Be strong and of good courage. Do not be afraid or dismayed . . . for there is one greater with us than with him. . . . With him is an arm of flesh; but with us is the Lord our God, to help us and to fight our battles.' . . . And the people took confidence from the words of Hezekiah king of Judah."

II Chronicles 32:7, 8

HEZEKIAH gave words of encouragement to his people. The Lord, he said, is with us. He will help us. He will fight our battles. And the people took confidence from the words of their king, or as one translation puts it, they rested themselves on his word.

There is rest for us in the words of our King. "Lo, I am with you always." "I will strengthen you, I will help you . . . ." "You will not need to fight in this battle; . . . stand still, and see the victory of the Lord."

What if the people had paid no attention to Hezekiah? What if they hadn't listened to his words?

Sometimes we are restless because we haven't been listening to the words of our King. Neglecting Bible study, we fail to hear our King speak to us.

Let the King speak to you as you read His Word today. What words of encouragement do you find? What words of help? Are there promises to claim?

Here is your source of courage and strength: "Resting . . . on the words of the king!"

BIBLE READING   *Psalm 36*
REVIEW MEMORY VERSES

JULY 7

"In peace I will both lie down and sleep; for thou, alone, O Lord, makest me dwell in safety."

Psalm 4:8

DAVID slept in many dangerous places. Many times he had enemies lurking near his bed. Yet he knew that he could rely on the Lord His God to make him dwell in safety.

Our only safety, waking or sleeping, is resting in the Lord and trusting in Him.

Perhaps you are on night duty, and trying to sleep in the daytime is hard for you. Rest in the Lord today. Ask Him to give you the sleep you need in spite of the interruptions and disturbances that are bound to come. Take His peace for your resting place this day.

BIBLE READING   *Psalm 37*
MEMORY VERSE   *Psalm 4:8*

JULY 8

"Trust in the Lord for ever, for the Lord God is an everlasting rock."

Isaiah 26:4

IN A WORLD where everything is changing rapidly it is good to rest the heart on the things which never change. Here are some of God's everlasting things for you to read:

An everlasting possession: *Isaiah 45:17*

An everlasting guide: *Isaiah 60:20*

An everlasting happiness: *Isaiah 35:10*

An everlasting love: *Isaiah 54:8*

An everlasting assurance: *Isaiah 55:3*

There is a solemn warning in Isaiah 33:14 for those who do not know the Everlasting God as their own Savior.

BIBLE READING   *Psalm 38*
MEMORY VERSE   *Isaiah 26:4*

" 'If it be so, our God whom we serve is able to deliver us from the burning fiery furnace; and he will deliver us out of your hand, O king. But if not, be it known to you, O king, that we will not serve your gods or worship the golden image which you have set up.' "

Daniel 3:17, 18

WALKING with God may sometimes involve dangerous adventures. But such adventures are always preceded by the kind of faith evidenced in these verses.

"God is able." "God will deliver us." "But if not, even if He doesn't, we will still obey His will for us."

God is the same today. We need Christian men and women whose faith will dare anything, knowing such a God as this.

BIBLE READING   *Psalm 39*
MEMORY VERSE   *Daniel 3:17, 18*

". . . and lo, I am with you always, to the close of the age. Amen."

Matthew 28:20

NURSES on vacation!
All the long days through,
You've a Friend who wants to spend
This summertime with you.

Nurses on vacation!
Listen and you'll hear
In the Word, from your Lord,
"Don't forget I'm near!"

Nurses on vacation!
Free to do your will . . .
Pray, heed your deepest need.
God is calling still.

BIBLE READING   *Psalm 40*
MEMORY VERSE   *Matthew 28:20*

JULY 11

"The fool says in his heart, 'There is no God.' . . . They . . . do not call upon the Lord."

Psalm 14:1, 4

AN ATHEIST does not believe in God. If you are living in sin and prayerlessness, you are an atheist as far as the practical results of your belief in God are concerned.

The fool in these verses may be saying quite another thing out loud. It is in his heart that he says, "There is no God." He may pray aloud, but from his heart he cannot call upon the Lord, for he doesn't really believe in Him.

Do you believe in God? Has your belief made any difference in the way you live? Do you spend time in prayer and in Bible study?

"No one," Jesus said, "cometh to the Father, but by me." Have you come to God by Jesus Christ? Is He your Savior from sin?

If we really believe in God, we will be seeking to understand His will and to please Him. And we will call upon Him from our hearts, to meet our needs.

Do you believe in God today? Have you said in your heart, "There *is* a God"?

BIBLE READING   *Psalm 41*
MEMORY VERSE   *Psalm 14:1*

JULY 12

"I sought the Lord, and he answered me, and delivered me from all my fears."

Psalm 34:4

FROM ALL my fears! He delivers me from my fears of yesterday with its weight of sin and failure which only He can forgive. He delivers me from my fears of today and its urgent needs which only He can meet adequately. He delivers me from my fears of the unknown tomorrows which only He, the perfect Counselor, perfectly understands.

He delivers me from my fear of making mistakes. "I, the Lord your God, hold your right hand; . . . I will help you," He says to me. He delivers me from my fear of the atom and hydrogen bombs. "But according to his promise, we wait, for new heavens and a new earth, in which righteousness dwells."

If you seek the Lord, He will hear you. He is waiting to deliver you from all your fears.

BIBLE READING   *Psalm 42*
MEMORY VERSE   *Psalm 34:4*

JULY 13

"Jesus said to him, 'If you can! All things are possible to him who believes.'"
Mark 9:23

READ Mark 9:14-29 today. What happened when the people saw the Lord? What was the result when they brought their problem to the disciples? What did Jesus tell the disciples to do? What is the importance of believing prayer? of fasting?

What practical lessons for your own life can you find in this account as you work with patients who need the Lord Jesus?

BIBLE READING   *Psalm 43*
MEMORY VERSE   *Mark 9:23*

JULY 14

"The Lord has heard my supplication; the Lord accepts my prayer."
Psalm 6:9

WHEN YOU COME to God through His Son Jesus Christ, He hears your prayer. When you ask according to His will He answers you. And until you see the answer to your prayer, the language of this Psalm must be yours: "The Lord has heard . . . the Lord accepts . . . ."

God is the Answer to all your needs. God is able to do more for you than you can imagine; His plans for you far exceed the plans you have made for yourself. He wants to make you "conformed to the image of His Son." Go to God with your problems, for advice, for help. Go to Him for real authority, for strength, for wisdom, for every need you have.

How much time have you spent with God this week? Has He heard your supplication, or haven't you been praying?

Spend time in prayer today.

BIBLE READING   *Psalm 44*
MEMORY VERSE   *Psalm 6:9*

JULY 15

"But as for me, I will look to the Lord, I will wait for the God of my salvation; my God will hear me. Rejoice not over me, O my enemy; when I fall, I shall rise; when I sit in darkness, the Lord will be a light to me."
Micah 7:7, 8

MICAH has been painting such a dark picture in the first part of this chapter that one almost expects him to write, "Therefore will I just give up!" But he doesn't, for he's learned that no matter how black the surroundings, there is hope for the children of God.

When you fall, when you sit in darkness, when you look to others and they fail you, when you find that all the dark world is disappointing, it is time to look away from everything else and wait for God.

"The Lord will be a light" to you.

BIBLE READING   *Psalm 45*
MEMORY VERSE   *Micah 7:7, 8*

JULY 16

"And he did not do many mighty works there, because of their unbelief."
Matthew 13:58

THERE IS NO victory when there is unbelief. There is no joy for the Christian who does not believe in the Lord Jesus for the present moment, the present difficulty.

He will do mighty works in you and for you, in your hospital

134

and nursing school, if you will believe Him. Believe that He is able to do for you what you cannot do for yourself. Believe Him enough to obey Him. Let every moment be met by the "Yes, Lord," of your loving obedience.

Your unbelief may be the obstacle in the way of God's working in your life and among your friends.

BIBLE READING *Psalm 46*
REVIEW MEMORY VERSES

JULY 17

"Afterward he appeared to the eleven themselves as they sat at table; and he upbraided them for their unbelief and hardness of heart, because they had not believed those who saw him after he had risen." " 'O foolish men and slow of heart to believe all that the prophets have spoken!' " " 'Did not our hearts burn within us while he talked to us on the road, while he opened to us the scriptures?' "

Mark 16:14, Luke 24:25, 32

OFTEN we are hard-hearted. We do not believe that the life of the Risen Lord Jesus is possible for us because we do not trust Him enough to believe His promises.

Often we are slow-hearted, slow to believe. It takes time and many experiences of His faithfulness before we trust Him enough to believe His promises.

Talking with Him and reading His Word will help us to trust and love Him enough to have a burning heart.

BIBLE READING *Psalm 47*
REVIEW MEMORY VERSES

JULY 18

"And he said to them, 'Why are you afraid, O men of little faith?' Then he rose and rebuked the winds and the sea; and there was a great calm."

Matthew 8:26

DOUBT AND FEAR always show lack of faith. The trusting heart remembers that the Son of God is Master of all life's storms.

Are the winds of trouble and worry beating on your life today? Are the waves of difficulty giving you a rough voyage?

Take the Lord Jesus into your heart and life. Let Him be the Master of all the circumstances of your day. Let Him take your sin and doubt and fear.

When He takes charge there will be peace: "a great calm." He may not still the storm, but He will always give you a quiet heart in the midst of the storm if you will let Him control.

Trust Him today to rule in every circumstance of your life. Have faith in Him!

BIBLE READING   *Psalm 48*
MEMORY VERSE   *Matthew 8:26*

JULY 19

"Then they cried to the Lord in their trouble, and he delivered them from their distresses; he brought them out of darkness and gloom, and broke their bonds asunder."

Psalm 107:13, 14

> HE bears my burdens, breaks my bands,
> Brings blessings new . . .
> Who takes my troubles in His hands
> Will hold me, too.
> And though my life right now is hard,
> And all my foes are grim,
> I'll stand on duty, stay on guard,
> Because I'm trusting Him.

BIBLE READING   *Psalm 49*
MEMORY VERSE   *Psalm 107:13, 14*

"For I know the thoughts that I think toward you, saith the Lord, thoughts of peace, and not of evil, to give you an expected end."

Jeremiah 29:11 (KJ)

GOD HAS thought about you. He has planned ways to make you more like the Lord Jesus. He's thought of a better future for you than you could ever imagine for yourself.

His thoughts about your life — profession, partner, plans — far surpass your own ideas about what circumstances ought to come your way. You can always trust God, whatever comes to you, for His thoughts toward you are thoughts of peace.

Take time today to think about God, the love He's shown you through His Son, and thank Him for thinking about you.

BIBLE READING   *Psalm 50*
MEMORY VERSE   *Jeremiah 29:11*

"For I decided to know nothing among you except Jesus Christ and him crucified."

I Corinthians 2:2

DETERMINATION is a good character trait. We are determined to do our best in nursing. We are determined to give our patients the best of care. We are determined to learn all we can about their needs so that we can serve them effectively.

We are usually determined to know something. But Paul is talking about being determined to know *nothing* . . . except "Jesus Christ, and him crucified." What does the crucified Jesus Christ mean to you?

Jesus Christ crucified means all the love of God to the lost world. Jesus Christ crucified means eternal life for all who will trust Him. Jesus Christ crucified means an end to our old lives of sin and the beginning of a new life in Him. Our crucified Savior means peace, happiness, victory, strength, wisdom. Knowing Him is enough to meet every need of your life.

Determine today not to know anything of yourself; pray that you may know only "Jesus Christ and him crucified."

BIBLE READING   *Psalm 51*
MEMORY VERSE   *I Corinthians 2:2*

JULY 22

". . . the mind of a wise man will know the time and the way."

Ecclesiastes 8:5

CAN YOU tell time on God's clock?   Read these verses to discover what time it is:

II Timothy 3:1
Psalm 32:6
Psalm 56:3
Hosea 10:12
Hebrews 4:16
I Peter 1:17

BIBLE READING   *Psalm 52*
REVIEW MEMORY VERSES

JULY 23

"And my God will supply every need of yours according to his riches in glory in Christ Jesus."

Philippians 4:19

GOD DOES NOT supply your needs according to your wants, or according to your resources, or according to the riches of your community, or according to the generosity of your family and friends.

God does not stop at supplying the part of your need which seems apparent to you, or the part of your need that others see, or the part of your need that is easiest to fill.

God does not supply your need according to some meager supply of grace which is apt to run out at any minute.

But He does supply *all* your need "according to His riches in glory in Christ Jesus." He provides a heavenly source of supply for all your earthly need.

And it is all by His Son, the Lord Jesus.

Claim this promise for your need today.

BIBLE READING   *Psalm 53*
MEMORY VERSE   *Philippians 4:19*

JULY 24

". . . for your Father knows what you need before you ask him."

Matthew 6:8

GOD knows what I need for my nursing day,
And He is willing to give
Whatever I lack as I live for Him,
For His is the life I live.
He is all that I need for my nursing day,
He is wisdom and power and light;
He gives me the strength for each difficult task
And the knowledge to do it right.
You can know Him too as a Christian nurse;
Whatever you have to do,
He knows what you need for your busy day,
And He's waiting to give it to you.

BIBLE READING   *Psalm 54*
MEMORY VERSE   *Matthew 6:8*

JULY 25

"Let all those that seek thee rejoice and be glad in thee: and let such as love thy salvation say continually, Let God be magnified."

Psalm 70:4 (KJ)

WHAT ARE YOU looking for in life? Happiness? Success? Marriage? Goodness? Love? Wealth?

All these things and more will never satisfy you without Jesus Christ. He is the way to God; He is the salvation of God to you. Bring Him your wants and wishes. Let Him take the desires of your heart and give you in their place His perfect will.

In every life, either one's self is magnified or one's Savior. If God is magnified, more important than all your wants and wishes, you will find real satisfaction; if you are seeking your own will, you will be frustrated and unhappy.

Jesus Christ can meet your need by bringing you to God. He can give you security. He can give you forgiveness, rest, peace and a home in heaven. Come to Him today.

Read these verses: Jeremiah 45:5a; Matthew 28:5; Psalm 27:8; Colossians 3:1.

BIBLE READING   *Psalm 55*
MEMORY VERSE   *Psalm 70:4*

JULY 26

"Whatever your hand finds to do, do it with your might."

Ecclesiastes 9:10

NEARNESS to the Lord Jesus implies nearness to difficulty, for He never took the easy way out of anything. He goes before you today with assurances of His love and power and care, and marks the way for you to follow. Follow Him rejoicing — not reluctantly.

And whatever you do for Him today, do it with all the skill and care you have. Even little things must be done well when they are done for Him.

Put your whole heart into your work for Him today.

BIBLE READING   *Psalm 56*
MEMORY VERSE   *Ecclesiastes 9:10*

"For I have come down from heaven, not to do my own will, but the will of him who sent me."

John 6:38

HE LEFT HEAVEN and came to earth to do the Father's will. He went to the cross to do the Father's will — to die for you and me. He works in us today "to will and to work for his good pleasure."

The Lord Jesus did not please Himself; He pleased His Father. In heaven we will please God and do His will at all times, but we can have a little of heaven now, seeking to please Him in everything here on earth.

Do His will today in the place He has sent you.

BIBLE READING   *Psalm 57*
MEMORY VERSE   *John 6:38*

"And Jesus answered them, 'Those who are well have no need of a physician, but they that are sick.'"

Luke 5:31

THE long dark hall is waiting as I make my rounds tonight.
Many needs I cannot see; I need a special light.
But I'm not making rounds alone.   The Lord is by my side,
Each moment I must look to Him and trust Him as my Guide.
The loneliest patients lie awake.   Dear Lord, I wish they knew
The privilege it is to walk the darkest ways with You.
Help me tonight to help them, Lord.   Speak in the words I say . . .
And let Your light shine through the dark as I make my rounds
    and pray.

BIBLE READING   *Psalm 58*
MEMORY VERSE   *Luke 5:31*

JULY 29

". . . how you turned to God . . . to wait for his Son from heaven, whom he raised from the dead, Jesus who delivers us from the wrath to come."

I Thessalonians 1:9, 10

WE'RE WAITING for Someone. We are expecting Him to call for us at any moment and take us to His home. We're ready for Him.

We're talking about Him. We're so glad He's coming! We're thinking about all we shall do when we're with Him.

We're dressed in our very best. We've left behind our old ragged clothes of malice and grumbling and gossip and meanness, and we are wearing tenderheartedness and meekness and longsuffering and goodness and faith. Yes, we're ready for Him.

We're not discouraged by the darkest sights in our world, because our eyes are looking far away to try to catch the first glimpse of His appearing.

We're waiting for Someone.

"Amen. Come, Lord Jesus."

BIBLE READING   *Psalm 59*
MEMORY VERSE   *I Thessalonians 1:10*

JULY 30

"For thou art an holy people unto the Lord thy God: the Lord thy God hath chosen thee to be a special people unto himself, above all people that are upon the face of the earth."

Deuteronomy 7:6 (KJ)

THE LORD has chosen you. Let the total aim of your life be to live "unto Him."

We give ourselves to Him, presenting our talents and our love "unto Him."

We give our plans to Him, knowing that our future is His who will one day take us "unto Himself."

Giving our time to Him, we find every moment worth living, lived "unto Him."

He calls us "unto Himself."

BIBLE READING   *Psalm 60*
MEMORY VERSE   *Deuteronomy 7:6*

"Then he said to them, 'Go your way, eat the fat and drink the sweet wine and send portions to him for whom nothing is prepared; for this day is holy to our Lord; and do not be grieved, for the joy of the Lord is your strength.' So the Levites stilled all the people saying, 'Be quiet, for the day is holy; do not be grieved.'"

Nehemiah 8:10, 11

KNOWING God brings gladness to the darkest day on earth. Every day is holy, sanctified by His presence and power for every moment. "This is the day which the Lord has made; we will rejoice and be glad in it."

You will be strong enough for any task when you are rejoicing in your God, for you will be ready to relinquish all claims on your own life. He will be able to rule and His strength will be yours.

Take the joy of the Lord for this day. Be happy in Him.

BIBLE READING   *Psalm 61*
REVIEW MEMORY VERSES

AUGUST 1

"But you shall receive power when the Holy Spirit has come upon you; and you shall be my witnesses in Jerusalem and in all Judea and Samaria and to the end of the earth."

Acts 1:8

ACCIDENTS, injuries, deaths
listed
in
long
columns of figures.

Histories, physicals, charts
filed
in a neat stack
in the library.

Patients,
row after row,
suffering;
only one nurse to help them?

Souls in the dark
needing God,
waiting.
Is there also a shortage
of Christians?

BIBLE READING   *Psalm 62*
MEMORY VERSE   *Acts 1:8*

". . . and proclaim liberty throughout the land to all its inhabitants . . . ."

Leviticus 25:10

WHAT DOES LIBERTY mean to you?

Perhaps you are thinking of slavery, and how the liberty of the free man contrasts with the life of the slave.

Perhaps you are thinking of civil, political and individual liberty, rights that belong to you as an American citizen.

Perhaps, you are thinking of John 8:32. The Lord Jesus said, "And you will know the truth, and the truth will make you free."

Remember that He also said, "I am . . . the truth," and, "If you continue in my word . . . ."

Liberty can mean to you freedom from sin, freedom from slavery to it. Liberty can mean to you that you are set free to love and serve the Lord Jesus Christ. He alone can set you free from your-self and your sin. Trust Him to set you free today. Then you can proclaim liberty to others by telling them about His freedom.

Remember that if you are not free in Christ, you are a slave to sin, for everyone who sins is a slave to his sin (John 8:34).

What does liberty mean to you?

BIBLE READING *Psalm 63*
REVIEW MEMORY VERSES

"The Lord recompense thy work, and a full reward be given thee of the Lord God of Israel, under whose wings thou art come to trust."

Ruth 2:12 (KJ)

IF YOU are looking for rewards for your work here in this world, you will be disappointed. Such rewards are transient, if they come at all.

Do not look for rewards from your patients; they are not always grateful. Look for the "full reward" from the Lord you trust, and you will be really satisfied.

Trust Him to make your work rewarding in itself. There is real joy in doing a difficult task for Him. He even makes drudgery easier!

Trust Him for this day.

BIBLE READING   *Psalm 64*
MEMORY VERSE   *Ruth 2:12*

AUGUST 4

"Remember that thou magnify his work, which men behold."

Job 36:24 (KJ)

YOU are a magnifying glass to make Christ large and real to the people who look at Him only through you. If you are turned toward Christ for everything, others will see Him through you. But if you are looking at your faults and troubles or the sins of others, you will magnify them and Christ will not be seen at all!

Ask the Lord to help you magnify Him today. Read these verses: Luke 1:46; Psalm 69:30; 35:27; Philippians 1:20.

BIBLE READING   *Psalm 65*
MEMORY VERSE   *Job 36:24*

AUGUST 5

"Let the words of my mouth, and the meditation of my heart be acceptable in thy sight, O Lord, my rock, and my redeemer."

Psalm 19:14

SOMETIMES we are anxious that our words and thoughts be acceptable to our friends more than to God.

If we are praying this prayer and living in obedient watchfulness, refusing the thoughts and words which are not of Him, we will find that we can be true witnesses for the Lord, our Strength and our Redeemer.

BIBLE READING   *Psalm 66*
REVIEW MEMORY VERSES

"Then my tongue shall tell of thy righteousness and of thy praise all the day long."

Psalm 35:28

KEEP YOUR TONGUE so busy with His praise that it has no time left to speak useless and wrong things.

Pray today for those you will meet who do not know the Lord Jesus. Pray especially for patients, doctors and other nurses in your hospital. Ask for wise words to be given you to speak to them about the Lord Jesus.

Pray that each Christian nurse may be a witness to the Lord Jesus in word and deed and attitudes day by day.

Ask, too, for wisdom to know when not to speak. Sometimes what is unsaid is as important as what is spoken, in the winning of a soul.

Speak of His praise today!

BIBLE READING   *Psalm 67*
MEMORY VERSE   *Psalm 35:28*

"I will go in the strength of the Lord God: I will make mention of thy righteousness, even of thine only."

Psalm 71:16 (KJ)

GOING in the strength of the Lord God precedes witnessing to His righteousness. If I am living in my own strength, I can't tell others what God can do. I won't know.

The topic of our witnessing must be His righteousness, not ours. That is why grumbling is such a poor witness. Grumbling implies that what God has allowed to be is not the very best for us today.

Even weak Christians can be clear witnesses when they go in the strength of the Lord God.

You can go in His strength today and mention His righteousness to others.

BIBLE READING   *Psalm 68*
MEMORY VERSE   *Psalm 71:16*

AUGUST 8

"I will meditate on all thy work, and muse on thy mighty deeds."

Psalm 77:12

WHERE DO YOU turn your thoughts when you have time to think about anything you wish? Do you think about yourself and your wants and wishes? Then you will be dissatisfied and unhappy. Do you think about others? Then you will be discouraged. Do you think about Jesus and all His work and His doings? Then you will have real joy.

From your thoughts come your words. If your meditation is a glad thought of your Lord, you will find it easy to talk about Him. If your thoughts are on yourself, you may be a dull conversationalist; if your thoughts are on others, you may be a gossip; if your thoughts are on the Lord Jesus, you will be a witness.

Thoughts of Him are a real source of joy. The Psalmist wrote, "My meditation of him shall be sweet; I will be glad in the Lord!"

Think of Him today!

BIBLE READING   *Psalm 69*
MEMORY VERSE   *Psalm 77:12*

AUGUST 9

"I will sing of the mercies of the Lord forever; with my mouth will I make known thy faithfulness to all generations."

Psalm 89:1 (KJ)

NOTICE that the Psalmist is careful to make known the Lord's faithfulness with his mouth. Your mouth belongs to the Lord Jesus. He wants your words as truly as He wants your life. Give yourself wholly into His control. Let Him use you as He wishes.

Let Him use your life to make your patients ask "Why are you so happy?" or "What makes you different?"

Then let Him use your mouth to answer them.

BIBLE READING   *Psalm 70*
MEMORY VERSE   *Psalm 89:1*

"Wherefore he is able also to save them to the uttermost that come unto God by him, seeing he ever liveth to make intercession for them."

Hebrews 7:25 (KJ)

IF you have never come to God by Jesus Christ, the Bible says that you are condemned, an enemy of God, in need of salvation. He is able to save you. He is able to save you to the uttermost . . . to the very furthest limit of your need. He is waiting to give you forgiveness and salvation. Will you come to God through Him today?

Jesus died for our sins. He rose again. He is living now, loving you, waiting for you to turn to Him. Will you let Him be your Savior, your Way to God?

Then you will say:

> He ever lives to pray for me!
> Before God's throne He stands,
> A Savior with the marks of love
> Upon His hands.
>
> He ever lives to pray for me!
> His blessing to impart
> He bears the needs of all my life
> Upon His heart.

BIBLE READING   *Psalm 71*
MEMORY VERSE   *Hebrews 7:25*

"Yea, before the day was I am he; and there is none that can deliver out of my hand: I will work, and who shall [hinder] it?

Isaiah 43:13 (KJ)

WHEN YOU GIVE yourself to God for His use, He makes you His witness. Then your witness is His work and no one can hinder it — not your inadequacy, for it is His power at work within you; not your failure, for He is your victory over anything.

He has this day planned for you. Before you meet any of its difficulties, He knows them and has made provision for you to have His strength for each of them.

Let Him use you where you are today as His witness.

BIBLE READING *Psalm 72*
MEMORY VERSE *Isaiah 43:13*

AUGUST 12

"We have sinned, and have committed iniquity, and have done wickedly, and have rebelled, even by departing from thy precepts and from thy judgments."
Daniel 9:5 (KJ)

A PRECEPT is "an order intended as a rule of action or conduct, a working direction." The will of God is to be our "working direction" until we are ruled by Him in everything we do.

Then we will meet the people He expects to touch through us. The things we do will speak of Him; and the words we use will be just right for the need He sees.

But departing from His rule of conduct and choosing our own rebellious will for our lives always leads to sin.

Follow His precepts today.

BIBLE READING *Psalm 73*
REVIEW MEMORY VERSES

AUGUST 13

"The Lord has done great things for us; we are glad."
Psalm 126:3

TODAY look up and list some of the great things God has done for you.

Psalm 31:19
Psalm 92:4, 5
Isaiah 19:20
Jeremiah 32:19

Matthew 5:12
Psalm 103:11
Hebrews 2:3
I John 4:4

Think of what these things mean to you and thank Him. Let your gratitude show in loving obedience to Him today.

BIBLE READING   *Psalm 74*
MEMORY VERSE   *Psalm 126:3*

AUGUST 14

"A man that hath friends must show himself friendly: and there is a friend that sticketh closer than a brother."

Proverbs 18:24 (KJ)

THINK FOR AWHILE today about the friendliness of the Lord Jesus. He was friendly enough to spend time with us in surroundings very different from His heavenly home, without criticism or complaint. He found us imperfect, full of sin and need, often unfriendly to Him. Yet He spent His life with us and at the end He showed His friendship by loving us "even unto death."

What about your friendliness? Are you accepting the friendship of the Lord Jesus, spending time with Him, trying to please Him by your loving obedience?

And are you showing friendliness to others who need Him? Love for Jesus Christ will show itself in love for others.

BIBLE READING   *Psalm 75*
MEMORY VERSE   *Proverbs 18:24*

AUGUST 15

"This is my commandment, that you love one another as I have loved you."

John 15:12

Do YOU LOVE the nurse with whom you work for Jesus' sake?

My student days were always hard.
Yet in my college dorm
There was one port in time of need,
No matter what the storm.
I found a friend across the hall.
Her smile was sweet and warm.

It wasn't what she said to me.
(I guess I knew she prayed . . .)
It was her loving way with folks
That never seemed to fade,
And such a friendliness about
The way she offered aid.

I learned to know the Savior then.
I'm sure I heard His call
Because I saw Him in a friend
Who loved me too, and all
His love I might have missed, but for
That friend across the hall.

BIBLE READING   *Psalm 76*
MEMORY VERSE   *John 15:12*

AUGUST 16

"In the year that King Uzziah died I saw the Lord . . . . Then I said, 'Here am I!   Send me.' "

Isaiah 6:1, 8

As A STUDENT nurse I had a vision of the Lord in a way that I had not seen Him before.   I saw His skill in creating and healing, and I began to realize His power.

152

In these years too I began to realize my own inadequacy in everything; the task was too great for me. And I cried, "Lord, I am a sinner and I live with those who are lost."

Then came the Lord Jesus with His blood and touched me, and I remembered the verse: "If we confess our sins, he is faithful and just, and will forgive our sins and cleanse us from all unrighteousness."

I heard His voice saying, "Whom shall I send to these patients and to these nurses and to these doctors who need Me?"

Then said I, "Here am I; send me."

BIBLE READING *Psalm 77*
MEMORY VERSE *Isaiah 6:8*

AUGUST 17

" 'You are my witnesses,' says the Lord, 'and my servant whom I have chosen, that you may know and believe me and understand that I am He. Before me no God was formed, nor shall there be any after me.' "

Isaiah 43:10

WHO ARE you? "I am a nurse in a hospital, caring for patients."

"You are my witness," says the Lord.

Why are you here? "So that I may be a good nurse, so that I may serve others, so that I may learn to understand the sick."

"That you may know and believe me and understand that I am He."

Under every purpose of your life as a Christian nurse is the great underlying purpose of God. He wants you to learn to know and believe Him; He wants you as His witness in any situation in which He may place you.

He has shown you His power by saving you and teaching you to know Him. Show Him your gratitude by being a real witness to Him where you are.

BIBLE READING *Psalm 78*
MEMORY VERSE *Isaiah 43:10*

AUGUST 18

"This people have I formed for myself; they shall show forth my praise."

Isaiah 43:21 (kj)

IT DOESN'T TAKE much teaching in anatomy and physiology to make us marvel at the perfection of the human system. We are amazed at its intricate interworking. We think of the eye and ear, the circulatory system, the fact that we go on breathing a renewed supply of oxygen 24 hours a day, 365 days a year, and the supply is constantly there. We marvel at the bones, the muscles, the nerves . . . and we say, "Behold, I am fearfully and wonderfully made, and that my soul knoweth right well!"

We are formed for a wonderful purpose too. We are to use what He has given us to show the praise of Him who formed us for Himself.

No wonder our bodies are so susceptible to our mental attitudes. No wonder unhappiness breeds so many kinds of illnesses. We are formed for His praise, and any other aim in life may make the machinery of our bodies work itself into sickness.

He made you for Himself. Let Him use you today.

BIBLE READING *Psalm 79*
MEMORY VERSE *Isaiah 43:21*

AUGUST 19

"And he said to them, 'Follow me, and I will make you fishers of men.'"

Matthew 4:19

HE SAID, Follow me, and I will make you fishers of men.
He didn't say, "I'll give you rod and reel,
Good flies, new fishing stuff
Until you feel that you're equipped enough
To fish for men."

A boy of ten,
Sometimes, with a bent pin
Can catch more fish than rich old fishermen
With all the tackle money can produce.
So what's the use
Of worrying over what He'll make of us?

Why fuss
About the kind of fishing we're to do?
To me, to you
He says, "I'll make you fishers."
Let no whim of mine
Keep me away from following Him.

—Reprinted by permission from
KODON, *Wheaton College*

BIBLE READING   *Psalm 80*
MEMORY VERSE   *Matthew 4:19*

AUGUST 20

" 'Fear not, nor be afraid: have I not told you from of old and declared it? And you are my witnesses! Is there a God besides me? There is no Rock; I know not any.' "

Isaiah 44:8

THE DISEASE of fear is always caused by the microorganisms of things we know about ourselves or our circumstances or about others; it is never brought on by what we know about God.

In this verse we have some tried and proven specific remedies for the disease of fear:

First, God has said it.

Second, He has said it to you.

Third, You are His witnesses.

Fourth, Since He is the only God, and He loves you, there is nothing at all to fear.

Take these remedies *q.s.* and *p.r.n.* He will give you a fearless peace as you trust Him. Then you will be His witness, a case study to show what His power can do!

BIBLE READING   *Psalm 81*
MEMORY VERSE *Isaiah 44:8*

AUGUST 21

" 'Even to your old age I am He; and to gray hairs I will carry you. I have made, and I will bear; I will carry and will save you."

Isaiah 46:4

THE ANSWER to the problem of geriatrics was old in Isaiah's time. Old age which leans on the strength of the Lord makes white hair "a crown of glory."

Ask the Lord to meet the needs of your elderly patients today. Ask Him for loving tenderness to care for them gently and carefully. Ask Him to give you wisdom and patience in meeting their requests and calming their fears.

Thank Him too for such a promise for your own future. And since you have such a secure future, trust Him to meet every problem of yours today!

BIBLE READING *Psalm 82*
REVIEW MEMORY VERSES

AUGUST 22

"But I am the Lord thy God."

Isaiah 51:15 (KJ)

I CAN'T be a witness for the Lord today because I'm only a student nurse and my life is too busy.

But I am the Lord thy God.

I can't be a witness for the Lord today because I'm in a college dorm and it's too hard for me to live for Him here.

But I am the Lord thy God.

I can't witness for the Lord today because I'm a busy graduate and have no time to study the Word or pray.

But I am the Lord thy God.

I can't attend Bible study groups or prayer groups because I'm a busy charge nurse, and life is just too full for me now.

But I am the Lord thy God . . . And I have put my words in thy

mouth, and I have covered thee in the shadow of mine hand . . .
Who art thou, that thou shouldest be afraid . . . ?

BIBLE READING   *Psalm 83*
REVIEW MEMORY VERSES

AUGUST 23

"The Lord God has given me the tongue of those who are taught, that I may
know how to sustain with a word him that is weary. Morning by morning he
wakens, he wakens my ear to hear as those who are taught."

Isaiah 50:4

How GRACIOUSLY the Lord Jesus spoke. His words were always
appropriate. He spoke to the lost about His Father and the lost
were found. He spoke to sinners about forgiveness and they
came to Him to be pardoned. He spoke to His disciples about following Him and their obedience is still known, these many years
later.

Yet He never spoke His own words, but the words that His
Father gave Him to speak. Morning by morning He listened to
the words of His Father.

This is your secret for speaking a sustaining word to the weary
ones for whom you care. Each morning let God speak to you.
Give Him your ear and He will speak into it words that will control and sweeten your tongue.

BIBLE READING   *Psalm 84*
MEMORY VERSE   *Isaiah 50:4*

AUGUST 24

"They thirsted not when he lead them through the deserts; he made waters
for them flow from the rock; he cleft the rock and the water gushed out."

Isaiah 48:21

WATER COULDN'T come out of a rock . . . but water did! God
brings a blessing from many an unexpected place . . . a gift of joy
and refreshment that you never suspected would come.

Even in the dust and heat of the desert, God's people did not suffer from thirst when He was leading them. Let Him lead you; then, no matter what your circumstances, you will be satisfied, following Him.

Your way may be dusty, rocky and difficult, but He is still able to bring blessings out of unexpected places.

Is He leading you today?

BIBLE READING   *Psalm 85*
MEMORY VERSE   *Isaiah 48:21*

AUGUST 25

"For we are his workmanship, created in Christ Jesus for good works, which God prepared beforehand, that we should walk in them."

Ephesians 2:10

STUDY Jeremiah 1:4-8 today.   When was Jeremiah's task planned for him by God?   Does God have a plan for your life too?   Can He use you now in His service, or must He wait until you are older and more experienced?

Who sent Jeremiah?   Who told him what to say?   To whom did he go?

Who will send you out to your appointed tasks?   How will you know what to say?   To whom is God sending you today?

Is it necessary to fear what people will say?

Why is it wrong to be afraid?

BIBLE READING   *Psalm 86*
MEMORY VERSE   *Ephesians 2:10*

AUGUST 26

" 'You are the light of the world.   A city set on a hill cannot be hid.' "

Matthew 5:14

THIS DOESN'T SAY "You should be," or "You may be" or "Some day you will be." It says, "You are."

What kind of light are you? A dim flashlight? A darkly shaded light with self and sin hiding the brightness of the Lord Jesus from those who need Him? Sunlight with so many clouds of unhappiness between you and the Lord Jesus that His joy doesn't show at all.

Or are you His light, clean for His use, close for His direction, empowered with His strength, glad with His joy, shining to glorify Him?

Be His bright clean witness today.

BIBLE READING   *Psalm 87*
MEMORY VERSE   *Matthew 5:14*

AUGUST 27

" 'For we cannot but speak of what we have seen and heard.' "

Acts 4:20

PETER AND JOHN had been with Jesus. They had learned that "There is no other name under heaven given among men by which we must be saved." And this Lord Jesus Christ was so wonderful to them that they couldn't help preaching and teaching and telling others about the things they had seen and heard.

They had seen His miracles of healing. They had listened to His Words. "For God so loved the world that he gave his only Son, that whoever believes in him should not perish but have eternal life." They had seen Him die, and they had seen Him alive again after His resurrection. They had heard Him say, "You shall be my witnesses." Of course they couldn't keep quiet!

You can know this Savior too today. There is no other way to God. There is no other Savior from your sins. There is no other way of forgiveness and peace. Let Him come into your heart and life today. He will make you a different person. And having seen and heard Him, you won't be able to keep from speaking of Him either!

BIBLE READING   *Psalm 88*
MEMORY VERSE   *Acts 4:20*

AUGUST 28

"Can two walk together, except they be agreed?"

Amos 3:3 (KJ)

THE LORD will walk with you today
If you will choose to walk His way . . .
But if you want to choose your own
You'll find that you must walk alone.
Your patients need His tender touch . . .
His love will help you, oh, so much!
Then let your life to Him be true . . .
Dear nurse, He wants to walk with you!

BIBLE READING   *Psalm 89*
MEMORY VERSE   *Amos 3:3*

AUGUST 29

". . . the day of small things . . . ."

Zechariah 4:10

OFTEN in the busy day of a student or graduate nurse there is no time for long conversations or testimonies. Often patients are too sick to listen to a long talk or to benefit by it if they could.

God uses the little loving word in winning colleagues' and patients' hearts to the Lord Jesus. Let the small things of your day be used for Him.

In even the smallest duties, He is with you to help you. Learn to acknowledge His presence and to pray as you work.

BIBLE READING   *Psalm 90*
REVIEW MEMORY VERSES

" 'for the place where you stand is holy.' "

Joshua 5:15

PRAY TODAY for nurses wherever they stand. Pray that each nurse may trust the Lord to lead today. Pray that she may realize that her place of service, today, is a holy place where God is working, too. Pray that the drudgery of difficult tasks may be lightened by faith in the Lord's presence.

Pray for patients, too. Ask that each individual may receive the nursing care that will meet his most pressing need today. Ask that patients and nurses may have open hearts toward the Lord Jesus.

Pray for wisdom for nurses in dangerous places. Pray for missionaries, that God will keep them from discouragement and show you how to help them as you pray.

You may serve God where you stand today. God lets us share His work by answering our prayers.

BIBLE READING   *Psalm 91*
REVIEW MEMORY VERSES

"The next day he [John] saw Jesus coming toward him, and said, 'Behold the Lamb of God, who takes away the sin of the world.' "

John 1:29

JOHN PERSONALLY saw the Lamb of God coming to *him* before he called others to behold Jesus.

First he saw Jesus as One who could remove his sin; then he told others about the Lamb of God who takes away all the world's sin.

That is our basis for telling others about the Lord Jesus. He must be real to us before we can make Him real to others.

Notice, too, that John called attention to the person of the Lord Jesus, not to himself at all. Andrew and Philip and Nathanael and Peter followed the Lord Jesus after that, with scarcely a backward look at John.

Is Christ so real to you that others can see Him in your life and words? Does your life make others want to follow Him?

BIBLE READING   *Psalm 92*
MEMORY VERSE   *John 1:29*

". . . who is a teacher like him?"

Job 36:22

STUDENT days are the days to learn
Over and over, wherever you turn,
The power of God to keep you sweet
And gladden your soul when you've tired feet.

Student days are the days to find
A loving heart and a learning mind,
A Friend in a God who understands
And blesses the service of nurses' hands.

Student days are the days to trust —
(A prayer and a verse for the times you're "fussed")
Days to discover you're weak, and then,
To learn His power all over again!

BIBLE READING   *Mark 1*
MEMORY VERSE   *I Peter 1:8*

SEPTEMBER 2

"But the people that do know their God shall be strong, and do exploits."
Daniel 11:32 (KJ)

DOCTORS AND NURSES need to know their patients. Nurses need to know the doctors and their individual preferences. Nurses need to know each other and how best to work with one another.

Nurses need to know the charts and the order book and the hospital rules.

Christian nurses need above all else to know their God.

In order to know Him well, it is necessary to spend time with Him. (We drift apart from friends we never see.) Set aside some time every day with your Bible, a notebook and a pencil, and determine to really get to know your God while you are in nursing school.

Stop right now and ask Him to help you learn to know Him better. He will be your strength for your nursing days.

Remember that He has revealed Himself through His Son, the Lord Jesus. You cannot get to know God apart from Him.

BIBLE READING   *Mark 2*
MEMORY VERSE   *Daniel 11:32*

SEPTEMBER 3

"So the king appointed an official for her, saying, 'Restore all that was hers, together with all the produce of the field from the day that she left the land until now.'"

II Kings 8:6

GOD'S RESTORING LOVE is shown by the way in which He restores the fruits of the Spirit in our lives when we come back to Him.

The fruit of the Christian life, "love, joy, peace, long-suffering, gentleness, goodness, faith, meekness and temperance" should be gathered daily. Bible study and prayer and fellowship with Him will help restore to you the fruit of the Holy Spirit which your life so needs.

Read John 15. What does it say about fruit? How much can we produce by our own efforts? Why?

BIBLE READING   *Mark 3*
REVIEW MEMORY VERSES

"For the Lord will be your confidence . . . ."

Proverbs 3:26

NEW NURSES often lack confidence about their work and gain it through experience. Christian nurses find in the Lord a special kind of confidence about their life. (Philippians 3:3).

To learn all that is involved in confidence in Him, see:

Isaiah 30:15
Acts 28:31
Ephesians 3:12
Hebrews 3:6
I John 5:14, 15
Psalm 27:3
II Corinthians 5:6, 8
Philippians 1:6
Hebrews 10:35

As you experience His presence and confide in Him, He will give you more confidence.

BIBLE READING   *Mark 4*
MEMORY VERSE   *Proverbs 3:26*

"Even there thy hand shall lead me, and thy right hand shall hold me."
Psalm 139:10

WHEREVER you are today, "even there" you may have the blessing and presence of the Lord Jesus with you. That is enough for every need, isn't it?

A place of reviling and persecution can be a place of refreshing. Read II Samuel 16:13, 14. A place of drudgery can be a place of discipleship. Read I Chronicles 4:23. A place of bitterness can be a place of blessing. Read Exodus 15:23-25. (Marah means bitter.) A place of death can be a place of decision and renewal. Read II Samuel 15:21. In fact, any place can be a place where you will hear His voice. Read Jeremiah 18:2.

Recognize His presence and power for the place where you are. "Even there" He will bless you.

BIBLE READING   *Mark 5*
MEMORY VERSE   *Psalm 139:10*

SEPTEMBER 6

". . . thou renewest the face of the earth."

Psalm 104:30 (KJ)

RENEWED! Are you tired of your life with its failure and disappointments and discouragements? Would you like to begin with a new one?

Knowing Jesus Christ as your Savior will never get monotonous. Everyday as you go on with Him you will find a refreshingly new outlook on life.

You can be "renewed in the spirit of your mind."

You can be "renewed day by day."

You can have "the renewing of the Holy Ghost."

You can "renew your strength."

Look up Ephesians 4:23; II Corinthians 4:16 ;Titus 3:5, 6; Isaiah 40:31.

Turn your life over to Jesus Christ today. Let Him renew it with His life in you. Let Him take charge of your failures and disappointments and discouragements. He can do what you can't do, and He knows what is best.

"Therefore if any one is in Christ, he is a new creation."

BIBLE READING   *Mark 6*
MEMORY VERSE   *Titus 3:5, 6*

"Thy shoes shall be iron and brass; and as thy days, so shall thy strength be."
Deuteronomy 33:25 (KJ)

WE ARE NOT PROMISED strength for this week or this year or even for a lifetime. We cannot depend on Sunday's sermon or Wednesday's prayer meeting to last all week, any more than we can depend on one or two meals a week.

"As your days . . . so your strength." Each day you must take time to claim the strength that comes from knowing God.

There is a translation which paraphrases Matthew 28:20, "Lo, I am with you all the days, and all day long" (Bishop Moule). Make this promise your own — not only for your life, but for your days, your moments. Take His strength for today's need.

BIBLE READING   *Mark 7*
MEMORY VERSE   *Deuteronomy 33:25*

"And now . . . saith the Lord . . . I spake unto you, rising up early and speaking . . . ."
Jeremiah 7:13 (KJ)

ONE OF THE EXCUSES nurses make for neglecting to spend time with God is that their lives are busy and interrupted.

Yet an hour alone with God in the morning can make all the difference between defeat and victory for the day ahead of you.

Perhaps it will help you to use the necessary will power to get up for a quiet time if you realize that the Lord Himself so loves His own that He speaks of "rising up early" to speak to them. Wouldn't you like to be awake and listening some early morning hour when He is calling you?

Remember, too, that a good quiet time begins the night before. Begin to prepare by going to bed at a reasonable hour so that you will be adequately rested!

BIBLE READING   *Mark 8*
REVIEW MEMORY VERSES

SEPTEMBER 9

"And whatever is needed — young bulls, rams, or sheep for burnt offerings to the God of heaven, wheat, salt, wine, or oil, as the priests at Jerusalem require — let that be given to them day by day without fail."

Ezra 6:9

DARIUS THE KING made a decree in Ezra's day concerning the people of God. Your King, the God of heaven, makes a similar decree for you.

What do you need? Are you in need of strength and determination for your day? Perhaps you need a new look at the Lamb of God who takes away your sin. Do you need a new vision of sacrifice, to offer your all to God once more? Think of His death for you.

Perhaps you need the wheat of the Lord Jesus, that Corn of Wheat who died to bring forth much fruit, to become the Bread of Life for your spiritual food today. Do you need to be reminded that you are the salt of the earth? Maybe you need new joy (of which the wine speaks), or a new dependence on the oil of the Holy Spirit to make your Christian life run smoothly for Him.

Whatever you need, here is the King's decree: "Let it be given them, day by day, without fail!"

BIBLE READING   *Mark 9*
REVIEW MEMORY VERSES

SEPTEMBER 10

"Evening, morning, and at noon, will I pray, and cry aloud: and he shall hear my voice."

Psalm 55:17 (KJ)

EVENING, morning and noon I pray,
Leaning on God for my nurse's day.
Morning and noon and eventide . . .
Keep me close to Your wounded side.
Morning, evening and noon, Dear Lord,
I pause to pray and to read Your Word.
Evening, morning and noon I bring
Myself as my daily offering.

Morning and noon and evening late
To You I look and on You I wait.
Morning, evening and noon, each hour
Wisdom, blessing, love and power
Come from God; and so I ask
All that I need for my nursing task.

BIBLE READING   *Mark 10*
MEMORY VERSE   *Psalm 55:17*

SEPTEMBER 11

"My voice shalt thou hear in the morning, O Lord; in the morning will I direct my prayer unto thee, and will look up."

Psalm 5:3 (KJ)

THE GOD OF HEAVEN, the Creator of the universe, wants to hear your voice.

Then let this be your daily practice: Talk to Him at the beginning of your day. Direct your prayer to Him as you think about who He is, what He has done, and all He has promised.

Look up into His face and listen. Look in His Word for what He has put there for you for today's need.

And if you begin like this, it will be easy to keep looking up to Him all day long.

BIBLE READING   *Mark 11*
MEMORY VERSE   *Psalm 5:3*

SEPTEMBER 12

"Be still, and know that I am God: I will be exalted among the heathen, I will be exalted in the earth."

Psalm 46:10 (KJ)

SIT QUIETLY in the presence of God just now. Realize that He is God, worthy to be exalted in your life as Lord and King. He can be exalted among non-Christians only through the glad testimony of quietly obedient lives.

Take time to be holy, speak oft with thy Lord;
Abide in Him always, and feed on His Word; . . .
Take time to be holy, be calm in thy soul;
Each though and each motive beneath his control;
Thus led by His Spirit to fountains of love,
Thou soon shall be fitted for service above.

William D. Longstaff

BIBLE READING   *Mark 12*
MEMORY VERSE   *Psalm 46:10*

SEPTEMBER 13

"But I will sing of thy power; yea, I will sing aloud of thy mercy in the morning: for thou hast been my defense and refuge in the day of my trouble."
Psalm 59:16 (KJ)

YOU DO NOT NEED to be a poet or a musician to make a song of praise to God. He loves to hear you thank Him for your own special blessings. No one else has had exactly the same experiences you have had. No one else can thank God for precisely the things you're especially glad about today! There are some things for which no one else can praise him. Stop now to do this.

Has He been your defense and refuge in trouble? Has He been merciful to you? Has He shown His power in your life? Praise Him today.

You may want to use a hymn book in your devotional time. Sometimes the hymns that others have written can be used to help you praise God.

Don't forget to praise Him. He listens for your praise.

BIBLE READING   *Mark 13*
MEMORY VERSE   *Psalm 59:16*

"So teach us to number our days, that we may apply our hearts unto wisdom . . . O satisfy us early with thy mercy; that we may rejoice and be glad all our days."

Psalm 90:12, 14 (KJ)

LET THE LORD be your teacher today. He will teach your heart to be wise and satisfied and rejoicing.

It takes time to "apply" your heart to learn from Him, just as your nursing courses take hours of preparation. Learn the "applied art" of being glad all day.

Pray today for unhappy Christians. Some are unhappy because of unconfessed sin. Some are unhappy because of worry about circumstances. They have forgotten to look to the One who rules their circumstances. And some are unhappy because they have not spent enough time with God, and so have forgotten how satisfying it is to know Him well.

As you pray, ask the Lord to teach you ways in which you can bring His joy into the lives of others today. Let Him teach you.

BIBLE READING   *Mark 14*
MEMORY VERSES   *Psalm 90:12, 14*

"It is good to give thanks to the Lord, to sing praises to thy name, O Most High; to declare thy steadfast love in the morning, and they faithfulness by night."

Psalm 92:1, 2

READING ABOUT nursing will never make you a nurse. You can study Anatomy, Nursing, and Pharmacology until you are an expert in textbook theory, but if you never care for a patient and put your knowledge into practice as part of the medical team, you cannot become a nurse.

Textbook theory is valuable, but it must be used.

Reading about spending time with God and praising Him will never give you any personal gladness and peace. You must put your knowledge into practice.

It's good to read about praising God. It's better to praise Him yourself. There are things for which you can thank God that David never thought about.

Put your knowledge into practice today.

BIBLE READING   *Mark 15*
MEMORY VERSE   *Psalm 92:1, 2*

SEPTEMBER 16

"How precious to me are thy thoughts, O God! How vast is the sum of them! If I should count them, they are more than the sand. When I awake, I am still with thee."

Psalm 139:17, 18

EVERY NURSE MARVELS at the way the human body is suited to its environment: the mechanism of blood clotting, the healing of a wound, the intricate layers of skin with all their protective functions.

That is God, thinking about your needs!

We marvel at the nervous system and at the complex miracle of the human brain. We, who cannot create a single living cell, see God daily thinking about us.

He thinks of us day by day all our lives.

How much time do you spend thinking about God?

Do you let Him control your thoughts?

BIBLE READING   *Mark 16*
MEMORY VERSE   *Psalm 139:17, 18*

SEPTEMBER 17

"Let me hear in the morning of thy steadfast love, for in thee I put my trust. Teach me the way I should go, for to thee I lift my soul."

Psalm 143:8

LEARN TO LISTEN for the voice of God. Hear the sound of His loving-kindness in the circumstances of your day. Hear His voice of guidance and of love.

I think it's significant that the sense of balance and direction is found in the inner ear. Spiritually, too, a healthy "inner ear" will be tuned to the voice of God; it only can give balance in spiritual living. The listener will also find God's direction for living day by day. Notice that there is a specific way wherein we should walk.

A disturbance of the fluid in the inner ear may cause dizziness. Some of us are so caught up in the whirl of busy living that we aren't able to hear God's voice in our inner ear. We're too busy!

Let God speak in your inner ear today.

BIBLE READING   *I Peter 1*
MEMORY VERSE   *Psalm 143:8*

SEPTEMBER 18

"Better is an handful with quietness, than both the hands full with travail and vexation of spirit."

Ecclesiates 4:6 (KJ)

THIS IS ONE way of saying that if you are too busy for God, you are altogether too busy. Who of us has not felt the need for extra hands and feet for the many tasks our nursing days demand?

Yet if you take time to fill your hand with God at the beginning of the day, with His Word, with His peace, with His quietness, before you begin the business of your day, your hands will be too full to hold the vexation of spirit that lies in wait for you.

You need His quiet before you go on duty. Fill your hand with the quietness of God today.

BIBLE READING   *I Peter 2*
MEMORY VERSE   *Ecclesiastes 4:6*

SEPTEMBER 19

" 'Take heart, daughter; your faith has made you well.' "

Matthew 9:22

> WHY? Why?
> But I don't see . . .
>
> It wasn't sight that made you whole.
> Not sight at all!
> Remember when you looked to Christ
> And heard His call?
> It was your faith that trusted Him.
> And when you'd fall
> It wasn't sight that picked you up.
> Not sight at all.
> . . . You don't see now.
> But you can trust,
> And on your knees
> You will be glad to leave it all
> To Him.
> He sees.

BIBLE READING *I Peter 3*
REVIEW MEMORY VERSES

SEPTEMBER 20

"Yea, in the way of thy judgments, O Lord, have we waited for thee; the desire of our soul is to thy name, and to the remembrance of thee. With my soul have I desired thee in the night; yea, with my spirit within me will I seek thee early: for when thy judgments are in the earth, the inhabitants of the world will learn righteousness."

Isaiah 26:8, 9 (KJ)

NURSES LEAD BUSY interrupted lives. When we plan an hour alone with God, our friends may drop in for just that time to visit or to ask for help.

Why not share your quiet time with the friend who drops in? God may have sent you that very person so that you could speak His word to her.

Be flexible enough to fit into God's plan for you. Don't let irritation spoil your usefulness.

If God permits interruptions, use them for Him.

BIBLE READING   *I Peter 4*
REVIEW MEMORY VERSES

SEPTEMBER 21

"And I will give thee the treasures of darkness, and hidden riches of secret places, that thou mayest know that I, the Lord, which call thee by thy name, am the God of Israel."

Isaiah 45:3 (KJ)

ONE NURSE I know gets up to meet God while it is still dark and the others who share her apartment are asleep. She finds rich blessing in her quiet time.

It's hard for some nurses to find a time and place to be alone with God, yet when they manage it they find "hidden riches" in His Word for them.

You will never find it easy to spend time with God! The Enemy of our souls doesn't want us to grow in the knowledge of our Savior. It may mean giving up time that you would rather spend in other things; you may end up at times in some very strange place.

But you too can find "treasures" if you will take time to be alone with God.

BIBLE READING   *I Peter 5*
MEMORY VERSES   *Isaiah 45:3*

"And . . . Evil-merodach king of Babylon . . . lifted up the head of Jehoiachin king of Judah, and brought him forth out of prison, and spake kindly to him . . . and changed his prison garments: and he did continually eat bread before him all the days of his life. And for his diet, there was a continual diet given him of the king of Babylon, every day a portion until the day of his death, all the days of his life."

Jeremiah 52:31-34 (KJ)

WE ARE ALL prisoners of doubt and fear and Satan until our King, the Lord Jesus, comes to set us free. He died to release us from our prison and oh, how kindly He speaks to us!

"Come to me, all who labor and are heavy laden, and I will give you rest." "I have loved you with an everlasting love; therefore I have continued my faithfulness to you."

He changes our prison garments (which are described in Colossians 3:5-9) to clothes fit for the King's table, and all the days of our lives He invites us to sit there with Him.

He also gives a diet to those whom He sets free too. He feeds your soul with His word, "every day a portion," all the days of your life.

Don't be a prisoner of sin any longer. Let Jesus Christ set you free. He died for you. He lives for you. He will give you perfect liberty.

BIBLE READING *II Peter 1*
REVIEW MEMORY VERSES

SEPTEMBER 23

"Great is thy faithfulness."

Lamentations 3:23

EVERY NEW DAY brings you opportunities to prove the faithfulness of your God. Every new day brings you the chance to be faithful to Him.

Faithfulness is not always seen by others. Your faithfulness today may be in very little things. (How very faithful the Lord Jesus is in planning the little things that give you joy!) Your faithfulness today may be letting the Lord control the thoughts you think.

Every day, spend time in the presence of your faithful Lord. He will meet with you. In all that you do and say, seek to be faithful to him.

Think of specific times when He has proved His great faithfulness toward you and thank Him.

BIBLE READING *II Peter 2*
REVIEW MEMORY VERSES

SEPTEMBER 24

"But when you pray go into your room, and shut the door and pray to your Father who is in secret; and your Father who sees in secret will reward you. And in praying do not heap up empty phrases as the Gentiles do; for they think that they will be heard for their many words."

Matthew 6:6, 7

FIND A QUIET place to be alone with God every day. We need a prayer closet, a place to change the attitudes and emotions that clothe our souls.

Shut the door to the crowding worries and sins and hindrances that would upset your time with God. Open a window toward heaven. Keep the door to earth closed. Spend time with your Father.

Pray only prayers that you really mean or you will find yourself using "empty phrases." Be specific. Be simple. God will answer you.

BIBLE READING *II Peter 3*
MEMORY VERSES *Matthew 6:6, 7*

SEPTEMBER 25

"And in the morning, a great while before day, he rose and went out to a lonely place, and there he prayed. And Simon and those who were with him followed him, and they found him and said to him, 'Everyone is searching for you.' And he said to them, 'Let us go on to the next towns, that I may preach there also; for that is why I came out.' And he went throughout all Galilee preaching in their synagogues and casting out demons."

Mark 1:35-39

READ these verses carefully. What example did the Lord Jesus leave us as to a time for daily prayer? Where was He praying?

Simon and the others must have been up early, too. What lesson do you think this may have for us as followers of the Lord Jesus?

What result of prayer do you find in these verses? Notice the word "us" in verse 38. He may use you in His work after you spend time with Him in prayer.

BIBLE READING 1 John 1
REVIEW MEMORY VERSES

SEPTEMBER 26

"And he appointed twelve, to be with him, and to be sent out to preach."
Mark 3:14

WHEN THE LORD Jesus chose His disciples, He called them first to be with Him, and then that they might go and preach. They had to be near Him so that He could send them where He wanted them.

When the Lord Jesus calls you to be His disciple, He wants you first of all to be with Him — with Him in a love for Him, with Him in obedience to His Word, with Him in love for others, with Him in His plan for saving the lost.

You can go about your unit with your hand in His mighty one. You can know that He is with you. And you can be with Him in all His plans and purposes for your life.

Then he will send you out to do His work.

BIBLE READING 1 John 2
MEMORY VERSE Mark 3:14

SEPTEMBER 27

"In those days he went out into the hills to pray; and all night he continued in prayer to God."

Luke 6:12

WHAT IS THE MOUNTAIN in your way? Discouragement? Defeat? Lack of understanding? Unkindness? Is it a mountain of ill health or anxiety or weariness?

Turn your mountain into a blessing by spending time on it in prayer. You'll get a different perspective when you get above the foot of your mountain. You will see a view of God's mercy and loving kindness, a glimpse of "the land that is very far off." You will see a stretch of green pastures and still waters.

In the days when people were plotting against Him, Jesus went up on a mountain and prayed all night. The next day He chose His twelve disciples.

You too can make right decisions and have peace in your heart. Ask Him to teach you to pray about the things that trouble you.

BIBLE READING *I John 3*
MEMORY VERSE *Luke 6:12*

SEPTEMBER 28

"I am their inheritance . . . I am their possession."

Ezekiel 44:28

THERE ARE PEOPLE in poor circumstances who are heirs to rich estates but who don't know it. One such "missing heir" turns up occasionally and the newspapers print the story.

The world is full of God's "missing heirs," those who could have all His riches for their own, but who live instead in ignorance and poverty.

God offers to give Himself to those who will come to Him through Jesus Christ, His Son. He will be your inheritance. You can belong to His family by confessing your sin and your need of Him and taking the Lord Jesus as your Savior. Then He will be your inheritance, your possession. And you will belong to Him.

Claim your inheritance. Tell God that you need Him. Take the riches that He offers you today!

BIBLE READING *I John 4*
MEMORY VERSE *Ezekiel 44:28*

SEPTEMBER 29

"Be patient therefore, brethren, until the coming of the Lord. . . . You also be patient. Establish your hearts, for the coming of the Lord is at hand."

James 5:7, 8

WE'RE USED to a hurried life on duty and off. Waiting seems a wasteful thing to do. That's why, while we are patiently waiting for the Lord Jesus, we are to spend the time in watchfulness and prayer.

"Establish your hearts . . . ." Keep steady and true, and spend time in earnest, loving Bible study every day. Then no sudden shock or change will disturb you, for your heart will be established firmly in the truth you know.

Wait with patience. He will reward you with His presence. He has promised to come back to make you like Him and to take you to be with Him forever.

Spend some time in His presence today. Let Him teach you to wait patiently for Him.

BIBLE READING *1 John 5*
MEMORY VERSE *James 5:7, 8*

SEPTEMBER 30

"Acquaint now thyself with him, and be at peace; thereby good shall come unto thee."

Job 22:21 (KJ)

BECOME ACQUAINTED with the Lord Jesus. Take time to read the Word of God. Take time to speak to Him in prayer, and to let Him speak to you. Don't be content with knowing about Him. Become acquainted!

He is your peace, and He will bring peace to your life. He died to set you free from the sin that ruins your chances for peace. Let Him take charge of your life and you will find yourself at peace.

"Thereby good shall come unto thee" . . . the good of sins forgiven, the good of peace with God, the good of answered prayer, the good of a happy life. And best of all, the eternal good of being with Him forever.

Become acquainted with Him.

BIBLE READING *Psalm 93, II John*
MEMORY VERSE *Job 22:21*

OCTOBER 1

"And he said to them, 'Come away by yourselves . . . and rest awhile.' For many were coming and going, and they had no leisure even to eat."

Mark 6:31

> LET me draw near to Your fireside, Father.
> Far from the world's busy mart,
> Quiet and still in the warmth of Your welcome,
> I would be warming my heart.
>
> Though she hath her fires, dying and chill ones,
> The world never quite understands
> The difference in warming the heart of a sinner
> And warming his hands.
>
> And so I come to Your fireside, Father.
> Home where Your face I can see.
> Warming my soul in Your love of Your loved ones,
> Kindle Your loving in me.

BIBLE READING   *Galatians 1*
MEMORY VERSE   *Mark 6:31*

OCTOBER 2

"Now these Jews were more noble than those in Thessalonica, for they received the word with all eagerness, examining the scriptures daily to see if these things were so."

Acts 17:11

THE BEREANS are described as more noble than others because their minds were ready and eager to hear what God had to say to them. I think they must have been ready-handed to do what He commanded, too.

182

They searched the Scriptures. They looked for the hidden truths that change lives. And they did it daily.

Christian nurses belong to a noble profession. But we can be more noble . . . by studying the Bible daily and being ready to obey God in anything.

BIBLE READING *Galatians 2*
MEMORY VERSE *Acts 17:11*

OCTOBER 3

"And these words, which I command you this day shall be upon your heart; and you shall teach them diligently to your children, and shall talk of them when you sit in your house, and when you walk by the way, and when you lie down, and when you rise. And you shall bind them as a sign upon your hand, and they shall be as frontlets between your eyes. And you shall write them on the doorposts of your house and on your gates."

Deuteronomy 6:6-9

HIDE the Word of God in your heart . . . love it. Teach it to others. Talk of the good things you have found in it. Make it affect your hands . . . do as it says. Make it rule your mind . . . think about it, study it. Let it control your home. And let it be a welcoming sign to guests.

BIBLE READING *Galatians 3*
REVIEW MEMORY VERSES

OCTOBER 4

"It is the bread which the Lord has given you to eat."

Exodus 16:15

READ Exodus 16:14-31 today. The manna will remind you of the Lord Jesus, the Bread of Life. It will also make you think of your daily food, the Word of God.

Like your daily Bible study, it was to be gathered fresh every day. Some of you read many chapters. Some of you read less. But everyone should read enough to gain food for his own soul.

Study the Word every day, and you will have something fresh and good to give to those who need it. And on Sunday the week's blessings will just overflow in praise and testimony as you worship the Lord Jesus.

Don't try to live on yesterday's manna. Find something new today!

BIBLE READING   *Galatians 4*
REVIEW MEMORY VERSES

OCTOBER 5

"Yea, thou art my lamp, O Lord, and my God lights my darkness."

II Samuel 22:29

As YOU READ your Bible today, ask the Lord to illuminate for you those passages that you find hard to understand. He is your lamp!

Ask Him to make you a shining light, to show others to Him. Pray that His Word will lighten your way and show you anything in your life that may be darkening the paths of others.

The world around you is dark, and when you get away from the Lord Jesus some of that darkness creeps into your heart. When He is the Lamp of your heart He makes the "darkness light around you."

BIBLE READING   *Galatians 5*
MEMORY VERSE   *II Samuel 22:29*

OCTOBER 6

" 'Blessed be the Lord who has given rest to his people Israel, according to all that he promised; not one word has failed of all his good promise, which he uttered by Moses his servant.' "

I Kings 8:56

IT's GOOD to work with nurses who keep their promises. It's important that the nurse who says she will give a medication will be careful to do it.

Our God is completely dependable. He is a Friend who keeps His promises to the letter. Not one word fails.

What promises of His can you quote? What promises do you find in your reading today?

Trust God to keep His promises to you.

BIBLE READING   *Galatians 6*
MEMORY VERSE   *I Kings 8:56*

OCTOBER 7

"Those who carried burdens were laden in such a way that each with one hand labored on the work and with the other held his weapon. And each of the builders had his sword girded at his side while he built. The man who sounded the trumpet was beside me."

Nehemiah 4:17, 18

BUILDING a Christian life in the midst of the busy world of medical science may be a dangerous work. Don't try to build unarmed.

The Sword of the Spirit is the Word of God (Ephesians 6:17). You need His Word in your heart and in your hand as you work for Him in your place of service, bearing burdens, building for God.

Sound the trumpet of a clear testimony. Read the Bible daily. Memorize verses to help you. Spend time with God in prayer. Build with a sword in your hand!

BIBLE READING   *Ephesians 1*
REVIEW MEMORY VERSES

OCTOBER 8

"And they read from the book, from the law of God, clearly; and they gave the sense, so that the people understood the reading."

Nehemiah 8:8

ARE YOU FAMILIAR with the words of the Bible so that you can make it known to others? Spend time in Bible study so that you will be able to read it distinctly. Spend time with a concordance and a Bible dictionary. Read and compare different versions.

Think about the different passages. Recognize the presence of the Holy Spirit as your Teacher. Let Him speak to your heart through the Bible verses you are reading.

You must know the sense of any passage yourself before you can make it understandable to others.

Read the Bible systematically. Read daily. Read thoughtfully and prayerfully. Ask God to teach you what you do not understand.

Then you will be ready with the answer when someone asks you what you believe and why.

BIBLE READING *Ephesians 2*
MEMORY VERSE *Nehemiah 8:8*

OCTOBER 9

"Teach me, and I will be silent; make me understand how I have erred."

Job 6:24

MAKE THIS the honest prayer of your heart as you read the Word of God today. You will be surprised at how many Scriptures speak directly to your own need if you will open your heart to the Word of God.

There is always something new to learn about ourselves. So that we won't become discouraged, there is always something new to learn about Him.

If your Bible is worn out by your careful study of it, you will not be so easily worn out by the load of your nursing duties.

Be teachable today.

BIBLE READING *Ephesians 3*
MEMORY VERSE *Job 6:24*

"And a ruler asked him, 'Good Teacher, what shall I do to inherit eternal life?' "
Luke 18:18 (Read Luke 18:18-23)

THE rich young ruler went away
In poverty from Christ that day.
He might have shouted down the years
Of Him who wipes away all tears;
He might have held a lasting trust
When all his gold had turned to dust.
He might have grasped, and held as his,
The wealth of all that Jesus is!
Yet, sorrowful, he went away,
A poor young ruler from that day.

BIBLE READING   *Ephesians 4*
MEMORY VERSE   *Luke 18:18*

"Receive instruction from his mouth, and lay up his words in your heart."
Job 22: 22

As YOU READ the Bible today, let each verse speak to your heart.

Receive it as His Word — not only to your mind, though it is good to have the mind trained to think of God; not only to the reason, though it is important to see the logical order and meaning of what you are reading; but to your heart, to the place of your affections, to the center of your life. Let God's Word speak to your heart.

Lay up His words in your heart too. Treasure them as valuable. Memorize them as words that can mean everything to you.

When you close your Bible today, ask yourself if you have treasured any of His Words in your heart as you have read. Are you more conscious of His love to you than you were before? Do you love Him a little more because of today's Bible reading?

Receive the Word from His mouth!

BIBLE READING   *Ephesians 5*
MEMORY VERSE   *Job 22:22*

OCTOBER 12

"That which I see not teach thou me: if I have done iniquity, I will do no more."

Job 34:32 (kj)

HERE IS ANOTHER prayer to help you as you read the Word of God. There are many things that we skip over lightly, verses that may be old to us because we've heard them so often.

Let God teach you to see the things to which you are blind because of your childhood training or your present environment. Let Him speak to you about something which has never before been brought to your attention.

Then if God shows you an error or a sin, put it out of your life and go on with Him to greater service and joy.

BIBLE READING   *Ephesians 6*
MEMORY VERSE   *Job 34:32*

OCTOBER 13

"Great peace have those who love thy law; nothing can make them stumble."
Psalm 119:165

READ as far as you can in Psalm 119, the longest Psalm, today. What are the results of obedience to the Word of God according to this Psalm? What names for the Word of God can you find? List the verses which are prayers. List the verses which tell of some resolve or decision. List the verses which tell of joy or rejoicing.

Are you enjoying the Word of God as David did? How much time have you spent with the Bible in the last ten days? How can you plan to read it more regularly in the future?

BIBLE READING   *Psalm 119*
MEMORY VERSE   *Psalm 119:165*

"And those who know thy name put their trust in thee, for thou, O Lord, hast not forsaken those who seek thee."

Psalm 9:10

PRAY TODAY for Bible study groups among nurses. Some nurses have never studied the Bible before. Some nurses who are studying the Bible do not know the Lord Jesus as their Savior.

Pray for the Bible study leaders among nurses. Ask God to give them wisdom as they work with His Word.

Pray for guidance and wisdom in your own life in helping to get other nurses interested in studying the Word of God.

BIBLE READING *Philippians 1, 2*
MEMORY VERSE *Psalm 9:10*

"Where the word of a king is, there is power, and who may say unto him, What doest thou?"

Ecclesiastes 8:4 (KJ)

SPEND SOME TIME every day in memorizing the Scripture. It's the Word of the King of kings and it is full of power!

Power to save souls and bring gladness to heavy hearts . . . power to overcome evil . . . power to make you strong for anything.

Let God be sovereign in every nook and cranny of your devious heart. When He is ruling all your thinking and doing, His Word will work miracles in your life and in the lives of those around you.

No one can question His authority, you see. He has every right to make His promises come true, and all power is His. "The Lord God omnipotent reigneth!"

BIBLE READING *Philippians 3*
MEMORY VERSE *Ecclesiastes 8:4*

OCTOBER 16

"Thy words were found, and I ate them; and thy words became to me a joy and the delight of my heart; for I am called by thy name, O Lord, God of hosts."

Jeremiah 15:16

I HAVE READ that when a Jewish child was learning to read, it was the custom to put a drop of honey on the first page so that the child could taste the honey and enjoy the reading. On every page of the Scripture there is a drop of sweetness: the sweetness of God's love for us, the sweetness of His Son, our Savior Jesus Christ.

The more we read in the Book of God, the sweeter it becomes to us. Is it the joy of your heart today?

As you read the Bible today, let the words speak to you of Jesus and His love for you. Rejoice in Him as you read of Him; let His Word be the joy of your heart.

BIBLE READING *Philippians 4*
MEMORY VERSE *Jeremiah 15:16*

OCTOBER 17

"Yea, he loved the people; all his saints are in thy hand: and they sat down at thy feet; every one shall receive of thy words."

Deuteronomy 33:3 (KJ)

I WONDER if Mary thought of these words as she sat at Jesus' feet and "heard His word."

I wonder if the Lord was remembering this passage when He said, "Mary hath chosen that good part which shall not be taken away from her."

Sitting at Jesus' feet always means hearing His words. He is alive today. He wants our presence near Him just as much as He wanted Mary to sit at His feet in Bethany.

You see, "he loved the people." And He still loves you and me.

BIBLE READING *Colossians 1*
MEMORY VERSE *Deuteronomy 33:3*

"Rejoice in the Lord always; again I will say, Rejoice. Let all men know your forbearance. The Lord is at hand. Have no anxiety about anything, but in everything by prayer and supplication and thanksgiving let your requests be made known to God. . . ."

Philippians 4:4-6

THE LORD is at hand. He is near, now. He wants to give you the joy in your heart that will enable you to rejoice always. He wants to give you the faith to trust Him so that you will have no anxieties. You won't worry.

God loves the world. He gave His Son the Lord Jesus to die, to take on Himself the sins of the world. You may have real joy and peace through trusting the Lord Jesus as your Savior. Is He yours?

The Lord is at hand. He's coming soon to make this old world new. Are you His child?

If you are His, you will be able to rejoice in Him no matter how dark the world around you.

BIBLE READING   *Colossians 2*
MEMORY VERSE   *Philippians 4:4-6*

"Wherewithal shall a young man cleanse his way? By taking heed thereto according to thy word."

Psalm 119:9 (KJ)

WHEN YOU COME in hot and tired from a long day or a long trip, isn't a bath a relaxing relief? It's a good feeling to be clean all over, and it makes us more attractive to other people, too.

Sin in a life, even hidden sin, makes us feel dirty. And in subtle ways the uncleanness of our hearts affects our relationships with others.

This problem was not new when David wrote the Psalms. It's an old one, today.

But the old answer is still effective. First, of course, avoid dirt. The dirty book, the dirty joke, the dirty thought . . . take heed! Then, if you sin, don't try to cover the sin from God and pretend it

191

isn't there. Face yourself honestly. (If you need a bath, you take one!) Spend time letting God's Word sink deeply into your heart and life. Confess your sin and ask God's forgiveness. Trust Him for cleansing.

Some stains are harder to remove than others. Some we do not see right away. God may use different experiences to show them to us.

What does God say about cleansing in I John 1:9?

BIBLE READING *Colossians 3*
REVIEW MEMORY VERSES

OCTOBER 20

"Now the Lord of peace himself give you peace always by all means. The Lord be with you."

11 Thessalonians 3:16 (KJ)

THIS PRAYER of Paul's was no form, no first century equivalent of "Sincerely yours." He meant it as a practical possibility for Christians. "Peace at all times in all ways" another version says.

Pray today that the Lord of Peace Himself will give you "peace always by all means." He can give peace in the hurried, harried life of the hospital unit. He can give peace when circumstances are anything but peaceful. He is the Lord of Peace: *your* Lord for today and always.

Pray for your patients and every patient for whom a Christian nurse is caring. Ask that each Christian nurse may bring the Lord of Peace into her work today.

BIBLE READING *Colossians 4*
MEMORY VERSE *II Thessalonians 3:16*

"Therefore comfort one another with these words."

I Thessalonians 4:18

WE WENT TO CALL on a sick man the other day, and a little German lady welcomed us. "I am so glad you have come," she said. "He gets so lonesome and I have to cheer him so often up!"

I think all of us need that "cheering so often up." And there is nothing quite so comforting and cheering as the words of Scripture.

For hundreds of years the Bible has spoken comfort to the sin-sick, the weary, the dying and the poor. When your patients are longing for comfort, this Book can usually give just the needed help.

And best of all the comforting words of Scripture is the glad promise that some day we shall be with the Lord Jesus forever.

BIBLE READING   *I Thessalonians 1*
MEMORY VERSE   *I Thessalonians 4:18*

" 'God is not a man, that he should lie, or a son of man, that he should re-pent. Has he said, and will he not do it? Or has he spoken, and will he not fulfill it?' "

Numbers 23:19

THE PROMISES of God are for you. They apply to your present situation.

God promises to give you eternal life through His Son, Jesus Christ. God promises to forgive your sins. He promises to make you His child. He promises to answer prayer. He promises to lead you "into all truth."

God will keep His promises. He is waiting for you to believe them.

Bring Him your sin for forgiveness. Tell Him your need and your loneliness. Let Him make you His child and answer your prayer. Bring Him your life for His guidance.

He is near you today. If you come to Him in the name of His Son, the Lord Jesus, you will find that His promises are true.

BIBLE READING   *I Thessalonians 2*
MEMORY VERSE   *Numbers 23:19*

OCTOBER 23

"So she gleaned in the field until evening; then she beat out what she had gleaned, and it was about an ephah of barley."

Ruth 2:17

GLEANING in the barley-fields in the heat of the sun is hard work. Your muscles grow strong and at the end of the harvest season you are tanned and healthy. At first though, you may find the work very tiring and may even grow faint with the heat of the sun.

It's hard work too to glean from the Word of God the precious grains of truth that are there for you. Keep at it though and don't quit. You will find that it will strengthen you until you become a stronger Christian than you have ever been before.

BIBLE READING   *1 Thessalonians 3*
REVIEW MEMORY VERSES

OCTOBER 24

"For Ezra had prepared his heart to seek the law of the Lord, and to do it, and to teach in Israel statutes and judgments."

Ezra 7:10 (KJ)

WOULD YOU like God to use you in your work, your school, your residence?

Follow the example of Ezra. He prepared his heart to seek the law of the Lord. He prepared to do and to teach what he found there.

You will need a willing heart. A clean, loving heart. Jesus Christ, who lives in your heart, will give you all you need to prepare your heart for His service. Trust Him to give you strength. Then in His strength (you cannot do it in your own) prepare your heart.

Begin regular Bible reading. Begin to obey in every detail as God shows you His will for you. Begin to love others enough to teach them what you have learned or are learning.

Then God will use you.

BIBLE READING   *1 Thessalonians 4*
MEMORY VERSE   *Ezra 7:10*

" 'And I have put my words in your mouth, and I hid you in the shadow of my hand, stretching out the heavens, and laying the foundations of the earth, and saying to Zion, "You are my people." ' "

Isaiah 51:16

ARE YOU AFRAID of giving a clear testimony to your Christian faith? Is it easier to go along with the crowd?

Boldness comes from knowing more about the One of whom you witness. As you learn how strong He is and that His strength is for you, you will be less fearful of your own weakness.

Hide God's Word in your heart and you will find His words easier to speak with your mouth. Spend time every day with His Word.

Then, trusting Him to speak through you, be His witness.

BIBLE READING   *I Thessalonians 5*
MEMORY VERSE   *Isaiah 51:16*

" 'And they come to you as people come, and they sit before you as my people, and they hear what you say but they will not do it; for with their lips they show much love, but their heart is set on their gain. And lo, thou art unto them as a very lovely song of one that hath a pleasant voice, and can play well on an instrument: for they hear thy words, but they do them not.' "

Ezekiel 33:31, 32

IT IS A SERIOUS thing to know God's will and to refuse to do it.

All of us know nurses who seem lovely as long as they are being supervised, but who scamp on their work when no one is looking. We have little respect for such people.

In your profession as a Christian, be sure that your heart attitudes are obedient to God as you study. If there is a point where you are not willing to obey God, stop there and ask Him to make you willing before you read further.

You can learn more truth only as you are obeying the truth you have already learned.

BIBLE READING   *II Thessalonians 1*
REVIEW MEMORY VERSES

OCTOBER 27

"Then he said, 'O man greatly beloved, fear not, peace be with you; be strong and of good courage.' And when he spoke to me, I was strengthened and said, 'Let my lord speak; for you have strengthened me.'"

Daniel 10:19

WHEN THE LORD Jesus was here on earth, many a weak, crippled body was made strong by His touch. Many a person weak with sin, even possessed by devils, was made well when Jesus came.

He is just the same today. He makes us strong when He speaks to us. He is our strength! That is why the Lord could say to Paul, "My strength is made perfect in weakness." No matter how weak you are, His strength can be perfect in your life.

Listen to Him speak to you through His Word and prayer today. His Word to you will make you a stronger, braver, more courageous Christian.

And the more you hear of Him, the more you will want to hear. "Let my Lord speak," you will say to Him, "for you have strengthened me."

BIBLE READING *II Thessalonians 2*
MEMORY VERSE *Daniel 10:19*

OCTOBER 28

"'I have manifested thy name to the men whom thou gavest me out of the world; thine they were, and thou gavest them to me, and they have kept thy word.'"

John 17:6

A NURSE who walks a floor of tears and grief
Must often read the loving Word of One
Who wept with sorrow for His people's sin.
Within
The Bible there is strength
For all a nurse's busy day.
There's wisdom, too, to say
To some sick lonely soul who weeps for sin,
"God's friendly door is open, dear,
Won't you come in?"

BIBLE READING *II Thessalonians 3*
MEMORY VERSE *John 17:6*

196

"O Ephraim, what have I to do with idols? It is I who answer and look after you. I am like an evergreen cypress, from me comes your fruit."

Hosea 14:8

WHAT ARE YOUR idols? Perhaps you worship professional skill or the money that buys comfort for you. Maybe your idols are cute clothes, a pretty face, friendships.

When you have met the Lord Jesus and He becomes real to you, your idols seem as dull and wooden as all idols really are. They give you nothing; they take from you everything you have.

He takes from you only your sin and your worthlessness. He gives you all He is. Spend time in His presence. He will make your life fruitful and happy.

BIBLE READING   *Psalm 97*
MEMORY VERSE   *Hosea 14:8*

"The good man out of his good treasure brings forth good, and the evil man out of his evil treasure brings forth evil."

Matthew 12:35

WHAT DO YOU VALUE most of all? What is the treasure of your heart?

Use the extra moments of your day to memorize Scripture verses. If you hide away such a treasure in your heart there will be no room for evil things.

"Thy word have I hid in mine heart, that I might not sin against thee" (Psalm 119:11).

BIBLE READING   *Psalm 98*
MEMORY VERSE   *Matthew 12:35*

"For I know whom I have believed, and am persuaded that he is able to keep that which I have committed unto him against that day."

II Timothy 1:12 (KJ)

I'VE placed my confidence in Him.
I, too, can say
The work He's given me to do
Until that Day
Is safe within His hands; my task
Henceforth: obey.

I've placed my confidence in Him.
So I can know
(Although the seed I'm planting now
May scarcely show)
He'll take the task He's given me
And make it grow.

BIBLE READING   *Psalm 99*
MEMORY VERSE   *II Timothy 1:12*

"Pray constantly."

I Thessalonians 5:17

JUST before you go on duty,
Stop to pray.
There is One who knows your patients,
And today
He wants you to bring them to Him
As you pray.

Just before you go on duty,
Ask His aid.
He who knows and loves and keeps you,
Light or shade,
Will give courage lest you fail and
Be afraid.

Just before you go on duty,
Listen, too.
God who knows the needs of nurses
Speaks to you.
Give up all you have and are to
Him anew.

Yes, before you go on duty,
Stop to pray.
There are needs you have not noticed,
And today
God is waiting near to help you
As you pray.

BIBLE READING *I Timothy 1*
MEMORY VERSE *I Thessalonians 5:17*

NOVEMBER 2

" 'Now therefore, I pray thee, if I have found favor in thy sight, show me now thy ways, that I may know thee and find favor in thy sight. Consider too that this nation is thy people.' "

Exodus 33:13

MOSES PRAYED, "that I may know thee." Paul's aim was "that I might know him" (Philippians 3:10), and the Lord Jesus prayed, "that they might know thee, the only true God, and Jesus Christ, whom thou hast sent" (John 17:3).

God answered Moses' prayer with a promise of His presence and rest. He answered Paul's prayer with a promise of sufficient grace for weakness. And God is answering the prayer of His Son every day as people come to know Him through the Lord Jesus, and as His own people become better acquainted with Him.

Do you know God through His Son, Jesus Christ? You may know Him if you will trust Him as your Savior from sin, as the Lord of your life.

"For God so loved the world, that he gave his only begotten Son, that whosoever believeth in him should not perish, but have everlasting life. . . ." "And this is life eternal, that they might know thee, the only true God, and Jesus Christ, whom thou hast sent" (John 3:16, 17:3).

BIBLE READING   *I Timothy 2*
MEMORY VERSE   *Exodus 33:13*

NOVEMBER 3

" 'But from there you will seek the Lord your God, and you will find him, if you search after him with all your heart and with all your soul.' "

Deuteronomy 4:29

SOME OF US do not find God when we pray because we seek Him half-heartedly. We pray for guidance, but what we really want is to be led in our own way toward our own goal. We pray for strength to witness, but what we really want is an excuse to be silent.

200

Sometimes we even pray for forgiveness when what we really want is for God to overlook our sin so that we may continue to please ourselves.

You see, really to seek God is to seek a Holy Person who wants to make us holy, pure in thought and word and deed. If we are willing to walk His way, He will lead us. If we are willing to forsake our sin and seek to please Him, He will cleanse and use us.

But we must seek Him whole-heartedly.

BIBLE READING   *I Timothy 3*
MEMORY VERSE   *Deuteronomy 4:29*

NOVEMBER 4

" 'Whatever you ask in my name, I will do it, that the Father may be glorified in the Son; if you ask anything in my name, I will do it.' "
John 14:13, 14

THINK OF THIS promise which God makes for your need today as a Christian nurse. If you are a loyal and obedient subject, the very thing which you need most is the thing He is waiting to do for you. Waiting . . . until you ask.

Do you remember another verse that says, "You do not have, because you do not ask"? (James 4:2).

Take time to claim this promise for your need today.

BIBLE READING   *I Timothy 4*
MEMORY VERSE   *II Samuel 19:38*

NOVEMBER 5

"And behold, the half was not told me . . . ."
I Kings 10:7

STUDY THE STORY of the Queen of Sheba and Solomon in I Kings 10:1-13. There is a picture in this chapter of the Lord Jesus and the believer. Look for it.

The Lord Jesus answers all your hard questions. He will listen while you tell Him all that is in your heart. There is nothing hidden from Him. The more we see of Him, the more we must stop to worship Him. We can bring gifts to Him, and He will accept them and use them.

Look at verse 13. Our King makes a similar promise to us in John 14:13.

BIBLE READING *I Timothy 5*
REVIEW MEMORY VERSES

NOVEMBER 6

"He said, 'Fear not, for those who are with us are more than those who are with them.' And Elisha prayed, and said, 'O Lord, I pray thee, open his eyes that he may see.' So the Lord opened the eyes of the young man, and he saw; and behold, the mountain was full of horses and chariots of fire round about Elisha."

II Kings 6:16, 17

WE NEED to have our eyes opened to the resources and power of God. We need to continue to pray and believe, even when fear has blinded our eyes.

The resources of the Christian are always greater than the resources of the world around him.

Ask God to teach you to depend on Him.

BIBLE READING *I Timothy 6*
MEMORY VERSE *II Kings 6:16, 17*

NOVEMBER 7

"And Jabez called on the God of Israel, saying, Oh that thou wouldest bless me indeed, and enlarge my coast, and that thine hand might be with me, and that thou wouldest keep me from evil, that it may not grieve me! And God granted him that which he requested."

I Chronicles 4:10 (KJ)

THE PRAYERS in the Bible can help you in your own praying.

What were Jabez' five requests? What was God's answer?

In what way could you pray for an enlarged field of service? How might God's hand be with you in your hospital?

God is just the same today!

BIBLE READING   *II Timothy 1*
REVIEW MEMORY VERSES

NOVEMBER 8

" 'But now I am coming to thee; and these things I speak in the world, that they may have my joy fulfilled in themselves.' "

John 17:13

JUST BEFORE He died on the Cross, the Lord Jesus prayed for you and me. Read His prayer today in John 17.

What requests did He make for Himself? What requests did He make for others?

Why did He pray that they might be one? Can you see His prayer being answered in your life? In what ways? In the lives of other Christians? In what ways? In the church? In what ways?

Ask Him to teach you to pray.

BIBLE READING   *II Timothy 2*
MEMORY VERSE   *John 17:13*

NOVEMBER 9

"And Asa cried unto the Lord his God, and said, Lord, it is nothing with thee to help, whether with many, or with them that have no power: help us, O Lord our God; for we rest on thee, and in thy name we go against this great multitude. O Lord, thou art our God; let not man prevail against thee."

II Chronicles 14:11 (KJ)

SOMETIMES we slip into the habit of thinking that if circumstances were somehow different, we might expect God to work. At the same time, we question that He is able to do anything in the particular situation in which we find ourselves.

Yet even in a college or hospital where you may be the only Christian, you may pray Asa's prayer!

BIBLE READING   *II Timothy 3*
MEMORY VERSE   *II Chronicles 14:11*

NOVEMBER 10

"The Lord is near to all who call upon him, to all who call upon him in truth."

Psalm 145:18

> DEAR God, You know my needs and cares
> And yet You listen to my prayers.
> You know the thoughts I cannot say.
> I feel Your presence when I pray.
> You lift, Lord, when I bow in prayer
> With burdens that I cannot bear.
> The friends I love, my family, too,
> Are still more precious unto You.
> Yours is the earth, the sky, the sea.
> You know the hungry heart of me.
> Almighty God, All-Just, All-Wise,
> Thank You for listening to my cries!

BIBLE READING   *II Timothy 4*
MEMORY VERSE   *Psalm 145:18*

NOVEMBER 11

"For they all wanted to frighten us, thinking, 'Their hands will drop from the work, and it will not be done.' But now, O God, strengthen thou my hands."

Nehemiah 6:9

ARE YOU DISCOURAGED by the ridicule of others, or by their concern for you? Does the task seem impossible, too hard, too big, too unsuited to your tastes and talents? Are you afraid that you are not strong enough to finish what you have begun?

Then it's time to pray Nehemiah's prayer: "Now, O God, strengthen my hands."

Nehemiah's God is your God, Christian nurse. He can strengthen your hands.

BIBLE READING   *Philemon, III John*
REVIEW MEMORY VERSES

NOVEMBER 12

"In my distress I called upon the Lord; to my God I cried for help. From his temple he heard my voice, and my cry to him reached his ears."

Psalm 18:6

I'M AFRAID I have to read this verse sometimes as though it said, "In my distress I just quit praying"; or, "In my distress I worked frantically and complained so loudly that God had no chance to speak to my distraught soul."

Not David! "I called upon the Lord," he wrote, and added triumphantly, "He heard!"

What do you do when you are distressed? Only God can really solve your difficulties. Only He can hear your prayer and do something about your need. Call upon Him in Jesus' name today. He will hear!

BIBLE READING   *Hebrews 1*
MEMORY VERSE   *Psalm 18:6*

NOVEMBER 13

"Lord, all my longing is known to thee, and my sighing is not hidden from thee."

Psalm 38:9

IT helps me to know that the Dear Lord knows
My deepest desires and weariest woes,
Knows how my heart aches for what is not,
Knows the black void of the emptiest spot.

I seek the solace of His own Hand,
For only the Lord can understand.
He knows the depth of my day's desire,
The temperature of each testing fire,
He knows my need ere I bend my knees . . .
For all my longing the Dear Lord sees.

BIBLE READING   *Hebrews 2*
MEMORY VERSE   *Psalm 38:9*

NOVEMBER 14

"Then wilt thou delight in right sacrifices."

Psalm 51:19

PSALM 51 is the Psalm for the penitent sinner. Read it today.

David had displeased God by his sin, but he returned to God and confessed his wrong-doing. He admitted his sin and his need for the restoring mercy of God.

Read verse 5. When did David begin to be a sinner? We are "born in sin." Each of us needs cleansing to make us fit for God's holy presence.

Look at verses 7-10. Then turn to I John 1:7. How are we made clean in God's sight?

Have you been cleansed by the blood of the Lord Jesus, who died for you? Bring Him your sin. He will make you whiter than snow; He will change your heart. Will you trust Him to give you His cleansing today?

BIBLE READING   *Hebrews 3*
REVIEW MEMORY VERSES

"Thus says the Lord, . . . 'Your prayer . . . I have heard.' "

II Kings 19:20

> I HEAR thee, frightened child. What you have prayed
> Is on my heart a burden too. I long
> To give you rest and peace, your sorrow laid
> Upon my heart, and in your soul a song.
> I hear thee, child. Believe me, for I love you,
> I will give the thing for which you have prayed.
> Only be patient. Trust your God above you
> Knowing I love you. Peace! Be not afraid!

BIBLE READING *Hebrews 4*
REVIEW MEMORY VERSES

"This also comes from the Lord of hosts; he is wonderful in counsel, and excellent in wisdom."

Isaiah 28:29

NOTHING can come to us except that which God sends or permits. The "this also" of this verse can apply to your situation today, wherever you are, whatever He sends you.

Have you a special blessing today? It is from Him. Have you a test to try your faith? "This also" is being allowed by Him for your good.

Trust Him to be "wonderful in counsel" in guiding you today whatever your situation. Trust Him to be "excellent in wisdom," as He works in your life.

BIBLE READING *Hebrews 5*
MEMORY VERSE *Isaiah 28:29*

NOVEMBER 17

"Hezekiah received the letter from the hand of the messengers, and read it; and Hezekiah went up to the house of the Lord, and spread it before the Lord."

Isaiah 37:14

TROUBLED LETTERS from home and friends . . . how they can destroy our peace. It's hard to be away from situations which we only hear about through letters, and it's hard to answer such troubled correspondence.

Take the letter and spread it before the Lord. Let Him bear the burden of it. Let Him show you how to answer it.

The Lord who is near you in your need is near your loved ones too.

BIBLE READING *Hebrews 6*
REVIEW MEMORY VERSES

NOVEMBER 18

" 'Before they call I will answer, while they are yet speaking I will hear.' "
Isaiah 65:24

GOD IS WAITING to hear you pray. He is so ready to hear you that He begins to answer before you call. He begins to answer while you are still speaking! He is prepared for any emergency.

Doesn't knowing how eagerly your Father wants to hear your voice make you desire to spend more time in prayer?

What a tragedy that we do not pray about everything.

BIBLE READING *Hebrews 7*
MEMORY VERSE *Isaiah 65:24*

"May the Lord fulfil all your petitions!"

Psalm 20:5

No ONE but God can fully know all your need, and none but He can satisfy completely. Before you pray to Him, He is planning for your good always.

> There is no limit to the things
> My God can do.
> And I am asking Him today
> For strength for you.
> I know that when the burdens press
> Too hard to bear,
> You'll feel Him lift the load.
> God answers prayer.

BIBLE READING   *Hebrews 8*
MEMORY VERSE   *Psalm 20:5*

" 'Call to me and I will answer you, and will show you great and hidden things which you have not known.' "

Jeremiah 33:3

No ONE but God could make an offer like this and be ignored. Few of us call on Him to show us things beyond our knowledge. We seem to be content with our ignorance.

Call upon Him. Ask Him to do for you more than you can understand. Ask Him to do in you that which you need most to have done. Ask Him to do through you the things He wants to have done.

Call upon Him. He will answer you. And you will be amazed at the things He will show you which you never knew before.

BIBLE READING   *Hebrews 9*
MEMORY VERSE   *Jeremiah 33:3*

NOVEMBER 21

"Enter His gates with thanksgiving, and his courts with praise! Give thanks to him, bless his name!"

Psalm 100:4

ONE THANKSGIVING time I walked by the Lake of Galilee, and I imagined that I saw in the sands the footprints of the Lord Jesus. Here and there were bloodstains, for His feet had been cut on the stones, and in the distance I saw a cross on a dark hill.

Then I began to give thanks.

I am thankful for a warm room. The Son of man had not where to lay His head. He asked for a drink from a stranger at a wayside well. I have clear running water always at my disposal. I am thankful for warm clothing, and I remember that they gambled for His garment at the foot of His cross. His friends forsook Him and His companion betrayed Him. I am thankful for many faithful, loving friends. I am thankful for joy, for good times and laughter; He was acquainted with grief for me. I have the trust, love and prayers of my family; the brothers of the lonely Savior did not believe in Him. I am thankful for health and the work of my profession; I am thankful for a Savior who was "wounded" and "bruised."

More than all, this Thanksgiving, I am thankful for the Lord Jesus who died on the cross.

BIBLE READING   *Hebrews 10*
MEMORY VERSE   *Psalm 100:4*

NOVEMBER 22

" 'Again I say to you, if two of you agree on earth about anything they ask, it will be done for them by my Father in heaven. For where two or three are gathered in my name, there am I in the midst of them.' "

Matthew 18:19, 20

YOU HAVE an appointment with the prayer-answering God. He will be where Christians are meeting to pray. Will you be there, too?

You don't need a large number of Christians to have an effective prayer meeting. Two are enough. Find a prayer partner in your school of nursing. Spend time with her in prayer. Claim the promise of the verse at the beginning of this meditation.

BIBLE READING   *Hebrews 11*
MEMORY VERSES   *Matthew 18:19, 20*

NOVEMBER 23

"And as he was praying, the appearance of his countenance was altered, and his raiment became dazzling white."

Luke 9:29

PRAYING CHANGES everything about us. It changes the thoughts of our hearts and, as a result, it changes the expression on our faces. Prayer clothes us with the atmosphere of Heaven, too.

Others will see in your life a glad reflection of your Lord Jesus if you are spending time with Him. Remember what they said about Peter and John — "they recognized that they had been with Jesus" (Acts 4:13).

You can honor Him best by spending time with Him. Then time spent for Him will be spent according to His will.

"They looked unto Him and were radiant." Does His radiance light your life?

His beauty in you will attract others to Him. As you pray, everything about you will be changed.

BIBLE READING   *Hebrews 12*
MEMORY VERSE   *Luke 9:29*

NOVEMBER 24

"When my soul fainted within me I remembered the Lord; and my prayer came to thee, into thy holy temple."

Jonah 2:7

ONE OF THE LAST things the Lord Jesus told his disciples before He went to the cross was to remember Him (I Corinthians 11:

23-26). Isn't it strange that any of us should ever forget Him? He loved us enough to leave Heaven to come to "the place of a skull." And he loved us enough to remember us with His presence and love every moment.

One of the most wonderful things about Him is that He forgives our forgetting, and even when we wander until our soul is faint, He hears our prayer.

BIBLE READING   *Hebrews 13*
MEMORY VERSE   *Jonah 2:7*

NOVEMBER 25

"The Lord is good, a stronghold in the day of trouble; and he knows those who take refuge in him."

Nahum 1:7

THERE ARE THREE thick walls to this stronghold in the day of trouble. The first is the wall of God's goodness, protecting you from all but that which will work for your eternal good. The second is a wall of His knowing: He knows you and all your need. He knows all about your environment and tastes and difficulties. And the third is the wall of your trust in Him.

No enemy can crash these walls. Hide yourself in the stronghold of the Loving Lord who knows you. Trust Him to protect you today.

BIBLE READING   *James 1*
MEMORY VERSE   *Nahum 1:7*

NOVEMBER 26

"And the stumblingblocks with the wicked . . . ."

Zephaniah 1:3 (KJ)

READ THE first 8 verses of Zephaniah 1 today. Does it surprise you to find among the wicked idolaters some whom you and I might not class as wicked at all?

"Stumblingblocks." Not active in any kind of work at all . . . just there in the way for people to trip over. They might even be in the right way, but if they are not advancing spiritually they are still stumblingblocks, causing others to fall.

And then in verse 6 we read about "those who have turned back from following the Lord, who do not seek the Lord or enquire of him."

Seek the Lord today. Do not turn back from following Him. And pray that you may not be a stumblingblock to anyone today.

BIBLE READING *James 2*
REVIEW MEMORY VERSES

"The Lord thy God in the midst of thee is mighty; he will save, he will rejoice over thee with joy; he will rest in his love, he will joy over thee with singing."

Zephaniah 3:17 (KJ)

SEE HOW the Lord loves you!

He is mighty . . . mighty to save. His power is great enough to change you and make you His child if you will trust Him.

He is willing . . . willing to save you. He so wants to save you that the Lord Jesus Christ died on the cross for your sins. He is so willing to save you that He has given you ten million blessings of light and food and shelter and clothing . . . blessed you with life and a mind to think of Him, a heart to love Him, eyes to read His Word.

Let Him save you today. Then He will rejoice, and you will rejoice with Him. Let Him have His way in your life today. He will joy over you with singing!

BIBLE READING *James 3*
MEMORY VERSE *Zephaniah 3:17*

"Then those who feared the Lord spoke with one another; the Lord heeded and heard them, and a book of remembrance was written before him of those who feared the Lord and thought on his name."

Malachi 3:16

THE LORD is listening. Do you speak to Him?
Speak then with fear
Lest what He hears you say will not be what
He waits to hear.

The Lord is writing. Do you think of Him?
Think of His Name . . .
The Everlasting God, the Mighty One,
Always the same.

The Lord is listening. Let your thoughts and words
Be often of
His grace, His power, His goodness,
And His love.

BIBLE READING   *James 4*
MEMORY VERSE   *Malachi 3:16*

NOVEMBER **29**

"And be strong, all ye people of the land, saith the Lord, and work: for I am with you, saith the Lord of hosts."

Haggai 2:4 (KJ)

BE STRONG. You can be strong with strength that is not your own, but His. The Lord wants workers among His people. There is so much to be done! The hours are long and the work is not easy, but God's presence is with you to strengthen you in everything you do for Him.

Be strong and work, for He is with you in your ward today. He knows the strength you will need and He is waiting for you to turn to Him to supply it for you.

Some of us read the verse as though it said, "Be strong and talk about your strength," or "Be strong and criticize the weakness of others."

You won't need to talk about your strength if you are busy in God's service. Your work will be so well done that it will witness to His presence with you. And you will be too busy to see that others are weaker than you, except as you are able to help them become stronger.

"Be strong . . . and work, for I am with you."

BIBLE READING *James 5*
REVIEW MEMORY VERSES

NOVEMBER 30

"And Jesus lifted up his eyes and said, 'Father, I thank thee that thou hast heard me.'"

John 11:41

SPEND TIME today in thanking God for answered prayer. Thank him for hearing your prayers. Thank Him for prayers that you have seen answered, and for the ones that He is going to answer. Be specific. Thank Him for the wisdom to know what to pray for; and thank Him for the Holy Spirit, who prays in you as you talk to your Father.

BIBLE READING *Psalms 94, 95*
REVIEW MEMORY VERSES

DECEMBER 1

"He made the stars also."

Genesis 1:16

HIS sky —
No dark unbroken emptiness.
"He made the stars also,"
Lights to reflect His brightness;
And thus
He thinks of His people.
Stars . . .

"I, Jesus . . . the bright and morning star."

"Whereby the dayspring from on high
Hath visited us,
To give light to them
That sit in darkness and in the shadow of death."

"He made the stars also."

BIBLE READING   *Luke 1*
MEMORY VERSE   *Genesis 1:16*

DECEMBER 2

"Fear not, for I am with you, be not dismayed, for I am your God; I will strengthen you, I will help you, I will uphold you with my victorious right hand."

Isaiah 41:10

A GOOD LEADER always gives a reason for an order when it is possible to do so. It is easier to work with students who know the reason for the task at hand.

Today you have two commands from the Lord: "Fear not, . . . be not dismayed."

And God gives you His reasons. Fear not . . . because I am with you, because I am your God; because I will strengthen you, because I will help you, because I will hold you up with my right hand!

Resolve that in His strength you will obey His commands to "fear not" and "be not dismayed" today.

BIBLE READING   *Luke 2*
MEMORY VERSE *Isaiah 41:10*

DECEMBER 3

"And I will lead the blind in a way that they know not, in paths that they have not known I will guide them. I will turn the darkness before them into light, the rough places into level ground. These are the things I will do, and I will not forsake them."

Isaiah 42:16

SEE WHAT the Lord promises you in this verse. New sight for the blind, new leading for the lost, new ways for wanderers, new paths for the followers, new light for darkness and a straightening out of the crooked things in your life.

This is the Savior's promise. The Lord Jesus who died on the cross for you wants to give you a new vision of Himself today. He wants to lead you. He wants to bring you back from your wandering to the shelter of His heart. He wants to make you His follower. He wants to make your darkness light. He wants to level out the rough places in your life.

Will you come to Him today? Bring Him your need and tell Him that you trust Him. Let Him do for you all that He wants to do.

BIBLE READING   *Luke 3*
MEMORY VERSE   *Isaiah 42:16*

DECEMBER 4

"I have raised Him up in righteousness, and I will direct all his ways: he shall build my city, and he shall let go my captives, not for price nor reward, saith the Lord of hosts."

Isaiah 45:13 (KJ)

GOD DIRECTED all the ways of the Lord Jesus because He was willing to be directed. Is God directing you in all your ways today?

How do you regard the will of God for your life? The following verses tell something about the attitude of the Lord Jesus toward God's will.

John 8:28, 29: Who taught the Lord Jesus? How much did He do in His own strength? How often did He do the things that pleased God?

John 14:24: Whose words did the Lord Jesus speak? By whom was Jesus sent?

Matthew 26:39: What was Jesus' prayer in the Garden of Gethsemane?

Matthew 3:17: What was the attitude of God toward His Son?

Consider your attitude toward the will of God in the light of the example of your Savior.

BIBLE READING *Luke 4*
MEMORY VERSE *Isaiah 45:13*

DECEMBER 5

"Thus says the Lord, your Redeemer, the Holy One of Israel: 'I am the Lord your God who teaches you to profit, who leads you in the way you should go.' "

Isaiah 48:17

THE LORD is your Redeemer, your Leader and your Teacher. He will take the circumstances of your life and teach you to profit by them. He will take the confusion of your wandering and give you the calm of knowing His leading.

Spend time in thinking about Him. Nothing is truly profitable apart from Him, knowing Him is the greatest profit you could have.

He became your Redeemer by purchasing you with His blood.

You belong to Him, for He has bought you. Let Him take full possession of every word and thought and wish. Let Him do with you as He chooses and you will rejoice in the path He picks out for you.

Trust Him to lead you. He will!

BIBLE READING   *Luke 5*
MEMORY VERSE   *Isaiah 48:17*

DECEMBER 6

". . . because of the Lord who is faithful . . . ."

Isaiah 49:7

YOU HAVE present joy "because of the Lord who is faithful." You can be what you should be because of Him.

His faithfulness can do for you what you cannot do for yourself. His faithfulness can make you faithful.

To be occupied with your *own* faithfulness is to walk like a man on crutches who is constantly watching his feet! Maintain good posture. Look to His faithfulness and He will keep you from stumbling.

Rejoice today "because of the Lord who is faithful."

BIBLE READING   *Luke 6*
REVIEW MEMORY VERSES

DECEMBER 7

" 'And I will make all my mountains a way, and my highways shall be raised up.' "

Isaiah 49:11

MOUNTAIN ROADS make driving difficult, but the scenery along them is worth the trouble. High in the mountains you can see great distances. Shacks that seemed ugly when you were close to them become picturesque little dots on a breath-taking landscape. Sometimes you get high enough to look down on the clouds.

Difficulties are like mountains. They seem hard to get over, but if you follow God's way through them they will give you glimpses of glory.

You can get above the troubles of your day by looking to the Lord. He wants to show you, through your circumstances, spiritual realities which you have not yet seen.

Let your mountains of difficulty bring you nearer to the heights of God's love. Thank Him today for His way through your mountains.

BIBLE READING   *Luke 7*
MEMORY VERSE   *Isaiah 49:11*

DECEMBER 8

" 'There is no peace,' says the Lord, 'for the wicked.' "

Isaiah 48:22

THE WICKED have no peace. Even a little wickedness in your heart will keep you unhappy and troubled. That is why Jesus died.

He came to take away all your sins, to make you clean and fit for God's presence. He came to give you the peace of purity, the peace of His presence in your heart and life.

Lack of peace is always due to sin. You may lack peace because you worry. You may lack peace because others annoy you. (Obedient hearts "love one another," and love is not annoyed.) Perhaps you lack peace because you are too busy to spend time with God each day, too busy to recognize Him in your life and in your work, too busy to seek His will.

Look for peace in Him today. Turn away from any sin which is keeping you from a peaceful life with the Lord Jesus. Let him cleanse your life and keep you clean.

BIBLE READING   *Luke 8*
MEMORY VERSE   *Isaiah 48:22*

" 'And she will bear a son, and you shall call his name JESUS; for he will save his people from their sins.' "

Matthew 1:21

ARE YOU STRUGGLING with a load of sin that gets bigger every day? Have you heard about the Lord Jesus but never quite found time to become acquainted with Him? Would you like forgiveness and the chance to start a new life, with His help?

Think about His name today. His name is Jesus, the Savior. He died for your sins. He wants to be your Savior and He will be, if you will trust Him. His name is Lord, the Ruler with the sole right to the throne of your heart. "If you confess with your lips that Jesus is Lord, and believe in your heart that God raised him from the dead, you will be saved."

Be saved today. Ask Him to be Lord of your heart and life.

BIBLE READING   *Luke 9*
MEMORY VERSE   *Matthew 1:21*

"For I, the Lord your God will hold your right hand; it is I who say to you, 'Fear not, I will help you.' "

Isaiah 41:13

I WAS out in the dark and I'd lost my way.
I was too frightened to think to pray.
I was too blind in the dark to see
A single step ahead of me.
Then, as only a Father could understand,
God reached down and took my hand.
And just the touch of His hand on mine
Made the stars in my darkness begin to shine.
He tenderly opened my eyes to view
The wonderful land He was leading me through.
Oh, only my Father can understand
How glad I am that He holds my hand!

BIBLE READING   *Luke 10*
MEMORY VERSE   *Isaiah 41:13*

DECEMBER 11

"To lead a life worthy of the Lord, fully pleasing to him, bearing fruit in every good work and increasing in the knowledge of God."

Colossians 1:10

CHRISTMAS TIME is a special time of bringing pleasure to others. We try to decide what our loved ones want most and give them just that. We plan holiday teas and parties for our friends. Sometimes we get so busy trying to please others that we forget the most important One to please.

Have you thought about the Lord Jesus, who left heaven for a manger and a cross, of whom it is written that He "pleased not Himself"?

Pleasing Him: how little it takes! He sees our least action of love, our least thought of His will, and is pleased. At this season of His birth, let's seek to please Him in all things.

We can please Him in "every good work." We can please Him by "increasing in the knowledge of God." And we can please Him by leading a life "worthy of the Lord."

Ask Him to teach you to please Him.

BIBLE READING   *Luke 11*
MEMORY VERSE   *Colossians 1:10*

DECEMBER 12

"To this end we always pray for you, that our God may make you worthy of his call, and may fulfil every good resolve and work of faith by his power. So that the name of our Lord Jesus Christ may be glorified in you, and you in him, according to the grace of our God and the Lord Jesus Christ."

II Thessalonians 1:11, 12

MAKE THIS your prayer for yourself and your loved ones. Pray that Christian nurses may not forget to pray for each other as these busy days go by.

Pray for your patients, that they too may know the blessings of the calling of God.

Is your faith working by God's power, triumphing over the temptations that come your way?

BIBLE READING   *Luke 12*
MEMORY VERSE   *II Thessalonians 1:11, 12*

DECEMBER 13

"He who says he abides in him ought to walk in the same way in which he walked."

I John 2:6

WHAT ARE YOU REMEMBERING, John, as you write these words? How did the Lord walk?

The aged John might think for awhile and then tell you . . .

"He went about doing good. He spent long hours in prayer. He did nothing for Himself, but all that the Father gave Him to do. He lived lovingly; He had compassion on the sick and weak and sinful. He was a friend of publicans and sinners."

If you belong to Jesus Christ, your life should show it. You too should be doing good. You too should spend time with God. You too should be governed by God's will. Your life should be loving and compassionate and friendly.

Do you abide in Jesus Christ? Do you so make your home in Him that He is the One who lives in you, making of you the kind of person you have wished you could be?

If you abide in Him, He will live His life in you, and you will more and more walk as He walked.

BIBLE READING   *Luke 13*
MEMORY VERSE   *I John 2:6*

DECEMBER 14

"Beloved, thou doest faithfully whatsoever thou doest to the brethren, and to strangers."

III John 5 (KJ)

I'M GLAD this commendation doesn't say "perfectly" or "beautifully" or "successfully." God commends faithful work; it is faithfulness that pleases Him — loyalty, as another translation puts it.

Be faithful then in your nursing, and do your very best for Him. Then God will be pleased and it is pleasing Him that matters most, no matter what others think about you.

It's not surprising, either, that the faithful worker is often the successful one in the long run. As you are true to God in little things, He will give you larger things in which to be faithful for Him.

BIBLE READING   *Luke 14*
REVIEW MEMORY VERSES

DECEMBER 15

"But you, beloved, build yourselves up on your most holy faith; pray in the Holy Spirit, keep yourselves in the love of God; wait for the mercy of our Lord Jesus Christ unto eternal life."

Jude 20, 21

BUILD UP your health with proper food and rest and exercise. Build up your knowledge with diligent study for your nursing courses. Build up your personality with all-round friendliness and helpfulness. Build up your profession by good nursing habits and careful nursing techniques.

And while you're building, don't forget the most important building of all!

Build with Bible study and prayer and obedient watchfulness so that sin does not mar your fellowship with God. Build with other Christians and help them build, too.

And build with constant dependence on the Master Builder, the Carpenter from Nazareth.

BIBLE READING   *Luke 15*
MEMORY VERSE   *Jude 20, 21*

"My soul followeth hard after thee; thy right hand upholdeth me."

Psalm 63:8 (KJ)

"HARD AFTER" is an old expression meaning near or closely after. It was when Peter was following "afar off" that he denied his Lord. The followers of the Lord Jesus need to keep close to Him, close enough to know His upholding power when the way gets rough.

When we fail to follow closely, we stumble and fall. You see, the followers of the Lord Jesus have chosen a hard way. He never took the easy way out, and neither will you, if you belong to Him. He will never let your way get so easy that you do not need Him to hold you up. He wants His followers to lean on Him all the way.

Spend time in prayer and Bible reading. Spend time in fellowship with God's people. Spend time in listening to the Lord speak to you. Be obedient to the voice of your Lord. Then you can say to Him with David:

"My soul followeth hard after thee."

BIBLE READING   *Luke 16*
MEMORY VERSE   *Psalm 63:8*

"Thanks be to God for his inexpressible gift."

II Corinthians 9:15

GOD'S GIFT . . . too wonderful for words, too good to talk about adequately. God has given His Son to be your Savior, for He died for you; He has given Him to be your Friend, for He rose again and lives in Heaven for you, soon to return to take you to be with Him forever.

You need not wait until Christmas to receive this gift. Put out your hand of faith and take the Lord Jesus as your Savior today. Let Him come into your heart with His joy and this will be the loveliest Christmas you have ever known.

You need this gift, for your sins have separated you from God;

Jesus Christ is God's offer of peace and forgiveness to lost men and women.

And when you have taken Him into your heart and life, He is the one Gift that you can give to others and still keep for yourself. Have you told anyone about God's gift this Christmas season?

BIBLE READING   *Luke 17*
MEMORY VERSE   *II Corinthians 9:15*

DECEMBER 18

"For you know the grace of our Lord Jesus Christ, that though he was rich, yet for your sake he became poor, so that by his poverty you might become rich."

II Corinthians 8:9

THIS IS A SPECIAL verse for nurses who won't be home for Christmas this year. You are working for the sake of others who are unfortunate enough to be sick at Christmas.

The Lord Jesus was away from Home, His wonderful Home in heaven, for more than thirty years. And He didn't go back Home for vacations. You see, He loved you; He wanted you to share His Home some day.

Give your time this Christmas to Him who for your sake became poor. Serve Him gladly this Christmas.

BIBLE READING   *Luke 18*
MEMORY VERSE   *II Corinthians 8:9*

DECEMBER 19

"I the Lord have called thee in righteousness, and will hold thine hand, and will keep thee . . ."

Isaiah 42:6 (KJ)

HOW OFTEN in our work as nurses do we need just such a Savior as this! He calls us to Himself and promises to keep us; then, so that we'll know how near He is and how He wants to help us, He promises, "I will hold your hand."

My way is planned.
God holds my hand.
He calls His own
To places lone
And then goes too
To see them through
I'm glad He planned
To hold my hand.

BIBLE READING *Luke 19*
REVIEW MEMORY VERSES

DECEMBER 20

"And she gave birth to her first-born son and wrapped him in swaddling cloths, and laid him in a manger . . . ."

Luke 2:7

THERE WAS NO sterile nursery for the baby Jesus. His mother had no careful nursing care for the delivery. His bed was a manger in a stable.

Look at the babies in your hospital nursery. Every precaution is taken to give them a clean environment. Then think how much God loves you, to let His Son be born in a place like that, to let sinful men ridicule Him and put Him to death.

"For God so loved the world . . . ."

BIBLE READING *Luke 20*
MEMORY VERSE *Luke 2:7*

DECEMBER 21

"And Mary said, 'Behold I am the handmaid of the Lord; let it be to me according to your word.' And the angel departed from her."

Luke 1:38

PAUL CALLED himself a "bondslave of Jesus Christ." Mary called herself "the handmaid of the Lord." The Lord Jesus came, "not to be served, but to serve."

I have read that servants in the Orient were trained to obey the hand signals of the mistress so that she never need speak to them. "As the eyes of servants look to the hand of their masters, and the eyes of a maid to the hand of her mistress, so our eyes look to the Lord our God."

You can be the Savior's handmaid in the place where you are today. Keep close to His hand and watch His signals. Serve Him in your unit or wherever you may be.

BIBLE READING *Luke 21*
MEMORY VERSE *Luke 1:38*

DECEMBER 22

"Then opening their treasures, they offered him gifts, gold and frankincense and myrrh."

Matthew 2:11

THE WISE MEN worshiped the Lord Jesus, bringing Him gifts. Wise nurses will worship Him too.

The wise men opened their treasures. What do you treasure that you could give to Him?

There is the treasure of a willing heart and the treasure of a skilful hand. There is the treasure of precious time and money and loving words. There is the treasure of our sympathy. Who knows the value of a tear? There is the treasure of a gentle and quiet spirit. (This "in God's sight is very precious.")

Give the Lord Jesus the treasure of yourself today. He will value your gift and use you for His glory.

BIBLE READING *Luke 22*
MEMORY VERSE *Matthew 2:11*

"When they saw the star, they rejoiced exceedingly with great joy."

Matthew 2:10

LET THE LIGHT of the real meaning of Christmas shine into your life today.

The Lord Jesus Christ left heaven to be born in Bethlehem, to grow up in poverty, to die on a cross for the sins of the world. He died . . . but He rose from the dead. And now He lives, offering you His forgiveness, His peace, His love, His friendship.

All you need do is accept His offer, and trust Him to give you His peace and rest and new life. Then you will have the joy of knowing the Lord Jesus in all your work today.

Think of the shining love of the Lord Jesus this Christmas. Let that love shine deep in your heart. Let this Christmas bring you into a new relationship with the Christ of Christmas.

BIBLE READING   *Luke 23*
MEMORY VERSE   *Matthew 2:10*

"For to us a child is born, to us a son is given; and the government will be upon his shoulder, and his name will be called 'Wonderful Counselor, Mighty God, Everlasting Father, Prince of Peace.' "

Isaiah 9:6

ONLY A FEW HOURS by air from where you are this Christmas Eve, a little baby is crying because he is sick and hungry. His parents will take him to the witch doctor, high on a cold mountaintop. They do not know how to feed him properly. They have never heard of preventive medicine. They love him very much, but their little boy will die. The witch doctor has no help for them. And they have never heard of the comfort of the Prince of Peace. You could teach the parents to feed the babies the right foods. You could give preventive injections so the babies would not die of measles and whooping cough. You could love the people for the Lord Jesus, and tell them about Him. Ask your Counselor, the

mighty God, if He wants to use you to be a missionary nurse somewhere in His needy world. Let your Father govern your life, and
your career will never be wasted.

BIBLE READING   *Luke 24*
MEMORY VERSE   *Isaiah 9:6*

DECEMBER 25

" 'Behold, a virgin shall conceive and bear a son, and his name shall be called
Emmanuel,' (which means, God with us)."

Matthew 1:23

> To HOSPITAL halls carollers come
> And sweetly sing of the birth of God's Son.
> Here, the dark drama of difficult death,
> There, the breaking of birth's new breath . . .
> Nurse, tell them firmly, "All is well!
> He is with us, Emmanuel!"
>
> Christmas has come, and a pensive tear
> Rolls down many a face this year
> When carols bring memories better forgot
> And patients lie longing for what is not . . .
> Speak clearly, nurse, of the life that wins . . .
> "He saves His people from their sins!"

BIBLE READING   *Luke 2, Matthew 1:23, Matthew 2*
MEMORY VERSE   *Matthew 1:23*

DECEMBER 26

"And the shepherds returned, glorifying and praising God for all they had
heard and seen, as it had been told them."

Luke 2:20

THE STAR and the angels were gone, and the shepherds had to return to the humdrum work of herding sheep. The high inspirational
moment doesn't last always . . . but God never changes! They

230

brought a glory back to their work after they had seen the Lord Jesus. They praised God for the privilege of seeing Jesus, and when they no longer saw Him, they trusted God to work out His purposes while they glorified Him in their own circle.

Seeing the Lord Jesus will make the humdrum tasks of your busy day meaningful; you need never leave Him behind! It isn't *feeling* that He is near you that brings a glory to your day, for you won't always feel His presence; but it is *knowing* that He is there, believing His promise, that will glorify God in your busy day.

BIBLE READING *Psalm 96*
REVIEW MEMORY VERSES

DECEMBER 27

" 'Worthy is the Lamb who was slain, to receive power and wealth and wisdom and might and honor and glory and blessing.' "

Revelation 5:12

As you worship the Lord Jesus today, think of Him as the Lamb of God, the Holy One who died for you. See Him on the cross, bearing your sins, loving you.

And as you think about that, you will know that He is worthy to receive all that you have, all that you are. He is worthy to receive the power of your hand, whatever you can do for Him. He is worthy to receive your riches, your possessions, the wealth of your love. He is worthy to receive your wisdom, the light of your understanding, the power of your reason. He is worthy to receive the strength of your youth, the honor of your worship, the glory of your very best for Him, the blessing of your every thought and wish and ambition. He is worthy.

He died for you. Will you live for Him?

BIBLE READING *Psalm 100*
REVIEW MEMORY VERSES

DECEMBER 28

"Great and marvelous are thy works, Lord God Almighty; just and true are thy ways, thou King of saints."

Revelation 15:3 (KJ)

> No CHANCE to speak?
> My heart can still sing
> The song of my great
> And marvelous King;
> Just and true
> His almighty power,
> And His my heart
> While I work this hour.
> When I cannot speak,
> My smile must tell . . .
> "My King is doing
> Everything well!"

BIBLE READING   *Psalm 101*
REVIEW MEMORY VERSES

DECEMBER 29

"Then I heard what seemed to be the voice of a great multitude, like the sound of many waters and like the sound of mighty thunderpeals, crying, 'Hallelujah!' for the Lord our God the Almighty reigns."

Revelation 19:6

SOME DAY the Lord will reign over all the earth. Some day no one will question His authority. It is your privilege to let Him be the Almighty God today in every area of your heart and life. Prove His power for that greatest need of yours. He has all power! Sing your alleluia of praise to Him by letting Him rule over all the kingdom of your heart.

Let the multitude of your thoughts praise Him. Bring "every thought into the captivity of Christ." Let the multitude of your minutes and hours, the multitude of the crowding tasks of your day, praise Him. In everything let the Lord Jesus rule.

Is He "Lord God omnipotent" in your life today?

BIBLE READING   *Psalm 102*
REVIEW MEMORY VERSES

" 'Surely I am coming soon.' Amen. Come, Lord Jesus!"

Revelation 22:20

Is EVERYTHING topsy-turvy in your life today? Is your world full of unhappiness and trouble and suffering and heartache?

In the midst of it all, isn't it good to know that the Lord Jesus is coming soon, coming to take His own to be with Him, coming to change us to be like Himself? Then, after a while, He will return to this earth with us and set it all right.

He is coming soon. Look at your days in the light of His return. Would you like to be living as you are living now, when Jesus comes? He may come today.

Keep watching for Him!

BIBLE READING *Psalm 150*
REVIEW MEMORY VERSES

"Behold, I come quickly."

Revelation 22:7 (KJ)

> COME quickly, Lord.
> These beds are always filled,
> And sickness mars the beauty You have willed.
> Come quickly, Lord.
>
> Come quickly, Lord.
> We weary of the deaths
> And sufferings and pains and labored breaths . . .
> Come quickly, Lord.
>
> Come quickly, Lord.
> We want so much to see
> Your loved ones well again, from sickness free.
> Come quickly, Lord.

BIBLE READING *Isaiah 40*
MEMORY VERSE *Revelation 22:7*